STACEY DOOLEY

on the frontline with the women who fight back

3 5 7 9 10 8 6 4

BBC Books, an imprint of Ebury Publishing
20 Vauxhall Bridge Road,
London SW1V 2SA

BBC Books is part of the Penguin Random House group of companies
whose addresses can be found at global.penguinrandomhouse.com

First published by BBC Books in 2018
This edition published by BBC Books in 2019

www.penguin.co.uk

A CIP catalogue record for this book is available from the British Library

ISBN 9781785942990

Printed and bound in Great Britain by Clays Ltd, Elcograf S.p.A.

Penguin Random House is committed to a sustainable future for
our business, our readers and our planet. This book is made
from Forest Stewardship Council® certified paper.

Contents

For my mother,

the first impressive woman in my life

Introduction

It's ten years since my mum picked up the leaflet and brought it home. It said, 'Do you like fashion? Do you like travel? Do you like shopping?'

Tick, tick, tick – I answered yes to all the questions.

'If you do, give this number a call.'

I called the number, not sure what to expect. 'I just saw your advert, can you let me know what the story is?'

'Yes,' a researcher told me, 'we're a production company and we're looking for six young consumers who are obsessed with fast, throwaway fashion.'

That was me. Back then I used to work hard, save up all my wages and go down to the Arndale at the end of the week, where I would buy as many clothes as possible with no real thought about what I was buying and who had made it.

'We're making a documentary about where your clothes come from and the consequences of your shopping,' the researcher went on. 'The process will take you to India, where you'll see for yourself how the garments are made and perhaps try making some yourself. What do you reckon to that?'

'It sounds awesome!' I said. The only place outside Europe I'd been was New York.

Then I had a moment of panic. I had just turned 19 and had no experience of how telly works. Wait, I don't think I'll have the money to go, I thought.

'Would I have to pay?' I asked.

'Oh God, no, we will take care of all the costs,' she assured me.

'OK, cool!'

'So, why don't I come to your house and have a chat about it?' she suggested. 'We can have a look at your wardrobe and take things from there.'

'Yes, no sweat,' I said. 'I'll swap shifts with someone and get the day off.'

I was working at Luton Airport at the time, selling perfume in duty free – Calvin Klein one week, Dior the next. I'd been there a couple of years and I loved it. Although it was never going to be a career, it was really easy and straightforward and I had loads of pals. I loved being with my girls.

The researcher came down on my day off. She seemed quite posh, like much of the telly crowd, to be honest. As I was showing her through my things, she said, 'I can't believe you've got so much stuff!'

I explained that I didn't really have any outgoings, so all my earnings went on shopping and holidays. I didn't have any responsibilities. I was a baby.

She started firing questions at me. Now that I understand how telly works, I imagine she was rubbing her hands in glee at my answers, because every time I opened my mouth a sound-bite popped out, unawares.

For instance, I had pair of leather Dior gloves that I obviously didn't need. I'd bought them in Selfridges.

'How much were the gloves?' she asked.

'They were £200,' I said. 'Oh my God, that's, like, £20 a finger!' I cringe now, but that was my world.

The expression on her face said, 'I've just found a contributor.'

When she left, she told me not to get my hopes up because there were thousands of people left to see. 'Realistically you probably won't be selected. Thank you for your time, blah, blah, blah.'

I wasn't listening, though. I'm going to India, I thought. There's just no way that they're not going to take me.

My mother gave me a lot of confidence as I was growing up. She went the extra mile to fuss me and tell me how brilliant and capable I was. 'You can achieve anything,' she'd say, and I believed her. She was fiercely loving and loyal.

Eventually I got a phone call saying, 'You're down to the last few, but the channel have asked me to explain to you that this is really going to be quite tricky. It will be very immersive and as real and close to the workers' lives as possible, so you'll be spending a month in sweatshops and you'll have to sleep under the sewing machines. You might see things that are quite upsetting. How do you feel about that?'

'Yes, no problem I can handle it,' I said.

I had no idea.

They invited me along to the production company to speak to the executive producer. Walking into the office was like entering a new world, a different life. The producer had his feet on the table and was on his Blackberry throughout the meeting. There were five other people in the room asking things like, 'Why do you think you'd be good for this?' They put me through the mill.

I got a phone call a few days later saying, 'We'd love you to come to India. How do you feel about that?'

My heart leapt. 'Really delighted!'

The next thing I knew I was on my way to Heathrow with my bags.

I didn't have a privileged upbringing, but I was very fortunate compared to a lot of people. I was brought up in Luton and for a long time it was just me and my mother. My father is dead now, but he was never on the scene. My mum sort of knew that was going to be the case, so I didn't take his name. That's why I'm Stacey Dooley – Dooley is my mother's name.

My father had his demons; our relationship was difficult and fractured. But I don't ever think, Poor me. I just feel blessed that I had my mother. She was such a great mum. She went above and beyond to make up for the fact I didn't have two parents. I was very lucky.

My mum is so badass, so rad; she's so, so lovely. Growing up, I never went without – and the reason I didn't was because for a long time she had nothing nice. She sheltered me from a lot of what was going on and it's only now that I'm an adult that I recognise what she did for me, and how ridiculous her finances must have been. She was working really shitty jobs, doing really shitty hours for shitty money, but she did it because she was my mum. I will always be eternally grateful for that. And perhaps I don't tell her enough.

We lived in a really crap flat for a long time. We only got out of there when my mum took a photo of me in my nappy holding a mouse that I'd found and sent it to the council. Then we were lucky enough to get a council house. Eventually she met a man – my stepfather, Norman – and they had a child, my sister. He's been a beautiful father to her and a great influence on me so it's all worked out, but it was hard for us. It was not OK for a long time. So I'm not from a kind of perfect 2.4-children family setup in any way, but I'm also not someone who feels hard done by. I think that's why I never try to be too judgemental and write people off.

I was a bit of a nightmare from the age of 13. My mum says it was like I woke up onc morning and turned into a devil. I was really wild. I had no interest in school; I found it boring. I remember thinking, I just don't want to do this.

I was the pits. I started bunking off and went robbing with my mates in town, stealing blue eyeliner and Morgan tops from Debenhams. If my mother had known half of the things I was up to, she would have killed me or had a breakdown. I was awful. She would have been so disappointed.

I left school at 15, didn't collect my GCSEs, didn't even do a lot of them, which is again really awful. I never went to college, never went to university. Never did anything like that. My first job after I left school was waitressing for £3 an hour.

I was a late bloomer for sure.

Going to India was huge. I soon realised that I'd underestimated what the trip was going to involve and the kinds of questions that were going to be thrown up as a result. It was surreal from the start: I was desperate for the loo when I got off the plane in Delhi, but when I got to the toilets there was just a hole in the floor. It's totally standard to me now, but it threw me the first time. I was thinking, How am I going to do this for the next month?

Leaving the airport, I was blown away by the colours, the smell and the madness of Delhi. I remember seeing a cow in the middle of the road and thinking how bizarre it was. 'Why isn't anyone moving the cow?' I wondered.

'Cows are sacred to Hindus,' someone explained. 'They are incredibly well respected here.'

But it's just getting in the way, I thought.

Meanwhile, I was trying to work out who all the characters were – from the TV crew to the other five other contributors – and we were being filmed all the while, which felt quite intrusive. It was hot, I was hungry. There was so much going on.

We were six incredibly fortunate, privileged people who were taken right out of our comfort zone and thrown into a tough, chaotic existence. The idea was that we would live alongside the garment workers whose lives and jobs we were going to share, so the taxi from the airport took us straight to one of the poorest areas of New Delhi, where we stayed with a factory supervisor and his family. Their home was super basic because they were earning just enough to survive.

The next day we went to the factory, where 4,000 workers were turning out 10,000 garments a day for British high-street stores. It was a far cry from a sweatshop, but we weren't prepared for how hard you had to work to earn less than £2 a day. There were so many rules and regulations. You couldn't get up from your seat or go to the toilet without asking permission first. You couldn't chat. You couldn't relax for a moment. It was a hard slog and almost impossible to live on the wages. Forget being able to afford the clothes we were making – you couldn't buy anything apart from the basics. When we went to the shops after the first day, a small deodorant cost more than a day's wages.

Things got harder as the weeks went by. We ended up working 15 to 18-hour days in hot, dirty factories and sweatshops. Sometimes we slept on the floor under the sewing machines. About halfway through the trip, I was really sick – so ill that I was on my hands and knees on the pavement. Our lovely fixer held my ponytail while I threw up on the streets of Delhi, thinking, Help, I'm going to die in India!

A month is a long time to be away from your family when you're young. OK, I wasn't a kid anymore but at 19 you're still trying to work out who you are and I felt homesick. We spent some time in Delhi and then the rest of the time in and around Mumbai, where we were taken to Dharavi – the largest slum in Asia at the time, where *Slumdog Millionaire* was filmed. It was filthy, with open sewers running through the streets, houses built on top of houses and people living in ruins. Some of the kids I met there were starving or had broken bones. Some of them were being forced to work 10 to 12 hours a day. It was horrific, beyond belief, and it hit me like a ton of bricks.

I was never a nasty or unkind kid up until that point, I just didn't really ever think about anything or anyone else, because my entire existence was Luton and England. Of course I saw kids living in poverty on the news and knew there were people in India and elsewhere who were struggling. But it felt so far away and so far removed from my life. It's not at the forefront of your mind until you're sitting in front of a skeletal, starving child whose hands are bleeding from the work she's being forced to do. At that point, you'd have to be a monster not to think, This is awful. What can we do collectively as decent human beings to stop it happening?

One day we visited a home for kids who had been rescued from sweatshops in Mumbai. There was one lad I'll never forget. He sat down and showed me a box that had all of his gear in it – everything he owned – which amounted to a couple of T-shirts, some colouring pens and a toy. He had nothing else. It wasn't something that worked well for television – that was it. He was only tiny but he was very matter-of-fact about his life. He didn't know where his mother was, his dad had given him away and he had been sewing for as long as he could remember. He was rescued from a factory where the manager beat him up. It was very, very tragic.

Listening to him, I felt overwhelmed. I started crying my eyes out, especially when I realised that it wasn't just an isolated case. It was the norm for loads of kids in this particular part of India. It sounds cheesy, but it was a lightbulb moment for me. Christ, I thought. We are so lucky back in the UK. I was already missing things like toilet roll, hot water and soap and food that isn't going to make you throw up. I was pining for home but then I thought, I've only got to do this for another three weeks; this is their reality.

I had so much and was so greedy – and yet I wasn't a bad person. I was at that age when you go to work, get your wages, go out on the Friday and probably come back on a Sunday; you've worn all your gear and you start again. Then suddenly I was shown a completely different world that I was a part of, without knowing it. Until then I hadn't thought about where my clothes were coming from or how they were made. Now I instantly started to look at things differently. It opened my eyes.

The first overriding emotion is guilt – a sort of Western guilt – because you think, I have so much and I am so unappreciative at times. You see these folks who have nothing, and they're so giving and they will include you in any way they can, despite everything. It makes you just feel terrible. You think: I'm so awful, I've got to change. I've got to learn from this, I've got to be more like you.

The crew made sure we had a hard time because they needed decent telly. I remember one of the lads kicking off big time while the cameras were on him. He was saying things like, 'This place is a shithole! You've done this on purpose. You want a reaction – well, here it is.'

It was so uncool. I was dying of embarrassment. He was saying it in front of the Indian people who all live there.

Mind you, we all had our ups and downs. If I watched the series back now I know I'd be cringing at myself, at this leery, gobby lunatic from Luton who didn't know how to respond or behave. I had some funky outfit choices going on as well but I really thought I looked the part. I remember thinking, Fucking hairstyle is brilliant. These outfits are great. I look awesome. But watching it back I know I'd think, Kill me now!

It's funny, because prior to going to India, I'd never had any real desire or aspiration to be on television. But while I was there I found I really enjoyed being filmed, going through the sequences, meeting the contributors and finding out about other people's lives. I learned so much.

Then I started noticing that every time the crew needed a piece to camera or an opinion, they would go to me. I can definitely do this, I thought excitedly. Perhaps they're going to ask me to do some more presenting after this!

Who did I think I was? I was really young and inexperienced! I had no reason to be so cocky.

The flight home was the longest I'd ever been on, and I had mad jetlag on my first night back at my mum's house where I was living at the time. I just couldn't sleep. I felt I'd been on an emotional rollercoaster. I lay in the bed thinking, That was all just so unbelievable!

I sat up. Here I am in my comfy bed, I thought, but what about the boy at the orphanage and the girl with the bleeding hands? The thoughts were rushing through my head: I want to do something to help them. I want to do my bit.

I racked my brains for ideas and then suddenly it came to me. My twentieth birthday was coming up; I would ask the kids at the orphanage to draw some pictures and I would auction them at my birthday party. We'll go for a curry, I decided. I'll give the curry house a couple of hundred quid and they'll put some food on. We'll sell the pictures and then we'll give all the money back to the orphanage, back to the kids.

I got in touch with the production company, and explained. 'I'd love to do this. Can you let me know how to get in touch with the orphanage?'

They were very supportive. 'We'd like to film it, if that's possible?'

'No problem,' I said.

We raised over £500 for the kids that day and I gave my birthday money too. It wasn't much, but I knew it would make a huge difference to the orphanage.

Meanwhile, I think my mum was thinking, What the hell is going on? Where has my devil child gone?

I went back to waitressing and started campaigning; I wrote to organisations and shops where I loved to spend my money. 'I've just come back from India,' I said. 'I am a consumer and if you want me to spend my money with you, you have to ensure that the workplace conditions of the people who make your clothes are up to standard.'

Quite who I thought I was, I don't know. I was writing to these multimillion-pound corporations, saying, 'If you want my business [which was probably about £40 a month] then you're going to have to tell me that you're not using children in your factories.'

Very few of them got back to me.

Then the production company rang to say that *Newsnight* had invited me on – my first live telly gig. *Blood, Sweat and T-Shirts* was being heavily trailed and I think the channel was quite excited about it.

'Yes, that's cool,' I said.

'Are you sure?'

'Of course.'

Obviously I had never watched *Newsnight*. I didn't have a clue about its style and tone, or how much of a hard time Jeremy Paxman gave the guests and politicians.

I rang my mum. 'Mum, I'm going to be on *Newsnight*.'

'What?!!' she spluttered.

'Yes, I'm going to talk about globalisation and our shopping habits and how we can change as consumers.'

'You're mental,' she said. 'Jeremy Paxman is going to tear chunks out of you! I think you'd better watch it before you say yes.'

I googled *Newsnight*. 'Hmm, I see.'

But I can't be a wimp, I thought. I feel fairly comfortable about what I believe, so I'm just going to say yes and see how it goes.

On the day, Georgina, one of the other contributors on *Blood, Sweat and T-Shirts*, and I were ushered into the studio. Paxman was very sweet to us – really lovely, in fact – but he seemed to think my name was Racey. 'I'm Stacey,' I said.

A little later, he called me Racey again.

I was thinking, Shit, don't get that wrong because we're about to go live and you're going to call me Racey.

Just before we went live, I said to him, 'Look, Jeremy, I know you can sometimes give people a hard time, but don't try it with me.'

He must have thought, Who on earth is this leery girl that they've wheeled in front of me?

But he leant over and winked at me and he said, 'I only give you a hard time if you're a politician.'

I really enjoyed it in the end!

Nothing much happened after that. I was broke, and I got a job working in a clothes shop, Jigsaw, in St Albans. Then I started working in a pub in the evening as well. At one point I had three jobs: I was working in Jigsaw, in another shop called the Dressing Room and at the pub.

I didn't mind it. It was always exciting when the deliveries came in and all the new gear arrived. I'd put something aside and then I'd have nothing left from my wages because I'd spent it all! I loved the camaraderie of working with the other girls and really enjoyed interacting with the customers. The best part was helping them sort out their outfits to go to their dos, their weddings and their christenings.

I sometimes miss working in a shop, even now. I was happy. But then Danny Cohen, the controller of BBC3 at the time, asked to see me, and obviously I jumped at the chance. He started things rolling for me.

'I found you quite inquisitive: you were asking questions and you weren't worrying about coming across as being stupid,' he said. 'You empathised, you sympathised. How would you feel about your own series?'

He was being very brave because I had no experience and was totally unqualified. But he took the risk and commissioned two 60-minute programmes about child labour.

For my first solo gig I went to the Ivory Coast to look at life for children on the cocoa plantations. The idea was that I had been so taken with the lad in the orphanage in India that now I would be looking at the child labour around the world.

It was a nightmare. Africa was on another level; so tough, so relentless. The conditions were horrendous – there were kids working all day to machete cocoa pods off the trees and some of them were missing limbs. Survival was a constant struggle for them. Ironically they had never tasted chocolate, the end product of cocoa, and they weren't into it at all when I gave them some to sample. They couldn't understand the fascination people have with it.

I lived with an amazing family – Suzanne and her nine children. They lived in mud huts literally hours away from roads and towns. It was incredibly rural and remote. I quickly grew close to them all, even though they all spoke French and my French was terrible. Suzanne was really beautiful; she was a loving, selfless woman living a simple, basic existence. I gave her a bottle of perfume when I arrived and it instantly became a precious possession.

Their first language was Swahili and it was really funny when they spoke it among themselves because whenever they said my name, they said it how I say it, in a Luton accent. So it would be 'Swahili, Swahili, *Stacey*.' Sometimes the crew couldn't contain themselves. They found it hilarious.

I remember asking Suzanne how many kids she had, when we first sat down to do an interview. 'I've got ten,' she said. 'Nine are black and one is white.'

'One is white?' I said.

She smiled. 'You are one of my babies now,' she said with total sincerity. 'You are here, in my home; you're one of mine.'

She was so maternal. When I gashed my knee and ankle one day she tried her best to fix me and sort me out. She even got out her precious bottle of perfume and tipped it all over the wounds.

'Argh!' I screamed. The pain was terrible.

The filming days were really long, tiring and hard but the evenings were blissful. One of Suzanne's sons, Paul, was trying to learn English; every night around the campfire we would go through the French-to-English dictionary and he would ask me how to say things in English. It was really back to basics.

One evening, Paul said to me, 'Can I come to England. Is it a possibility?'

Oh no! I thought, I can't promise you anything. The likelihood is that you'll never leave this place.

'You never know what's going to happen, who knows?' I said, feeling sad for him. His dream was to get out of his depressing circle of poverty, go to a place like England and be able to earn real money.

A few days into the trip, I started feeling quite ill. I couldn't swallow. My tummy was upset. I felt weak and feverish. I tried not to worry, because everyone was saying, 'There's no way it's malaria, man; it's too quick. Malaria takes at least nine days.'

'OK, cool,' I said, trying to play it down. I thought they wouldn't want to work with me again if I got sick on the first ever trip for the show.

The next day we met a Lebanese family who owned a massive cocoa factory in the economic capital, Abidjan. The father had private health care and he sent his son to my hotel to see if I was OK.

The son turned out to be quite handsome. When he asked about my symptoms, I felt embarrassed telling him I had the shits. On top of everything else! He sent along their doctor who did a blood test and diagnosed malaria. What are the chances? On my first solo job? I was so unlucky.

I now know many people who have had malaria, but at the time I thought it was a death sentence. No! This is awful! I thought. I'm going to die, I'm going to die in Africa. In the drama of the moment I threw my arms around the director, who wasn't a particularly emotional or tactile person. 'Get the hell off me!' he snapped. Poor guy – he's actually a good friend now.

I was taken to the nearest hospital and put on a drip. Everyone around me was speaking French. I lay in bed that first night feeling desperately sorry for myself. It was a night of real ups and downs. At one point a baby was born in the next-door room. I could hear it crying and the mother was so, so thrilled that her baby was fine. Meanwhile I felt really frightened and alone, going in and out of consciousness, convinced I was on the verge of dying. When you're that ill, you don't know what is real or if you're hallucinating, and whether you're making any sense. It was really bizarre. I've never felt so ill.

When I didn't respond to the drip, the insurers flew me in an air ambulance to Ghana, where at least they spoke English. 'Don't tell my mum because she'll go loopy,' I told everyone. 'She will be so concerned that she'll drive herself insane.'

There was a flashing ambulance waiting for me when the aeroplane landed in Ghana and I was rushed to a hospital in Accra. After that, I seemed to hear Celine Dion singing 'My Heart Will Go On' everywhere I went – in the hospital, in the hotel, in the car. It was on loop throughout the entire country and I thought, Christ, if malaria doesn't kill me, this song will.

When I got a bit stronger, they flew me to London. Our fixer went back to Suzanne and her family and said, 'She's not being rude. She's just not very well. They're going to fly her back in a few weeks to continue the filming.'

Suzanne was so concerned about me that she sent Paul to a market hours away on his pushbike to buy a phone card so that they could ring to see how I was doing.

'Suzanne has used her life savings to buy this phone card because she wants to know how you are,' the fixer told me when he rang.

Wow, what a woman! I thought. How can you care so much for somebody that you've just met? How can you be willing to part with everything you own, literally, to make that call? What about that?

It took a couple of months to get better and then I went back to the Ivory Coast to finish the documentary. 'Stacey, my baby!' Suzanne cried out when she saw me.

She was incredible, so kind – your archetypal earth mother.

For the first few years doing telly, I was still working in pubs and in shops, because I wasn't earning loads. It was only two or three weeks filming here and there. That was how it worked out for the first few years, until I was about 25.

People were really surprised when they came into the pub and I served them. 'I think I've seen you on telly, haven't I?'

'Yes, you probably have,' I'd say.

'Why are you working here?' they'd ask. There's always an assumption that as soon as you're on the screen you're rolling in money.

'I'm broke – that's why I'm working here,' I'd laugh. 'I need to pay my rent.'

I moved out from my mum's a few years after I got back from India. Then I moved back. Then I moved out again, until slowly I became a bit more settled. Now I've got a flat that I share with my boyfriend, Sam, and my dog, Bernie – and a job that takes me all over the world.

Looking back, I always think, Thank God I answered that advert! Thank God my mother showed it to me! Thank God Danny Cohen was at BBC3 at the time, because he changed my whole life. Sometimes I can hardly believe it happened, but the fact is that in the last ten years I've made more than 50 documentaries – 70, if you count the films I've made for CBBC. I've achieved more than I could ever have dreamed of.

I'm under no illusion: I know my life would be completely different if it wasn't for *Blood, Sweat and T-Shirts* and Danny Cohen. I would probably still be in Luton, which isn't a bad thing, but I would never have travelled as much as I have, seeing the world and witnessing things from other people's point of view. Politically, I might have even voted differently to how I do now, and I think my crowd of friends would have been very different. My morals, my ethics and everything I've been through has shaped me and turned me into the woman I am now – but it started with my trip to India, no doubt.

My work has definitely made me less self-obsessed. I'm not perfect – I am still quite vain and love fashion and spend lots of money on myself – but I think I'm a lot less judgemental now, and a lot more open minded and reflective. If I hadn't left Luton I don't think I would have grown in the same way – travel is such a brilliant way to challenge yourself and make you think.

On my trips to hostile environments and the poorer parts of the world, I've seen that when people are having a tough time, the women are always up against it that bit more than the men. And that's why I started to focus on the experiences of women around the world in my work. Suzanne in the Ivory Coast was one of the first females who really inspired me – her life was so hard, but she was so strong.

Now, after a decade of making documentaries, it seems like a good time to shine a light on some of the incredible women and characters I've met over the years by collecting their stories into a book. A lot of the women I've focused on have gone through the mill – they've been knocked down so hard that it's hard to believe they've got up again. But they haven't given up – they keep on going, keep on fighting. It's so inspiring.

The girls and women I've met on my travels in the last ten years have completely moulded me – there's no question – and I'm so grateful, because they've given me a sense of awareness I wouldn't have had otherwise. Seeing into their lives helps you keep your priorities in check, and that's something you can't buy. It's something that comes with experience and age; it's a learning process.

I've never for a moment thought that single-handedly I could fix things that have been broken for such a long time. But if nobody knows about what's going on, nothing can change. So in my mind I've got to be the woman who stands up and has something to say. Because I want to be able to look at myself in the mirror and think, I've been true to what I believe in. I've said my bit.

You have to be a strong fierce female. The world is tricky and I think if you don't fight for what you believe in – if you don't try and be the change that you want to see, however cheesy it sounds – what's the point? Especially as we live in a country where you're able to do that without being thrown in jail or persecuted. You have the right, you have your voice – as long as you're not inciting hatred, you can say whatever you want. Sadly, that's not the case for so many girls and women across the world.

Thank you for buying this book. I hope the stories and issues you read about will help to inform and inspire change.

Just by knowing about them, you're helping.

1

Tiffany, Sharon, Nicole and Danielle

Prison

In the summer of 2012, I flew to America to make my first series of *Stacey Dooley in the USA*, which was a bit of a turning point for me. Although I had already worked on several solo documentaries, until then I hadn't been massively involved editorially. I was just a presenter and still learning.

My first documentaries were very different from what I'm making now, partly because I didn't narrate them – instead the producers brought in a male narrator to provide the commentary. I suppose they thought I didn't have enough credibility to voice the entire film, and in hindsight I agree.

They were thinking, We need an authoritative voice here!

But as I learned more about how television works, I became more capable and comfortable in the job and got more involved in the editing. So I started saying, 'It's ridiculous that it's not my voice narrating, because it's my journey. It's my experience.'

I pushed and pushed until gradually I was allowed to start commentating.

I don't blame the producers for being cautious. Critics were saying that my style was a bit clumsy – and they were absolutely spot on, because it was very clumsy at the start. It was sincere, and there was a real interest and a real appetite to learn and understand, but I didn't know what I was doing, because I wasn't a trained journalist. I hadn't studied media, so I was very unorthodox, and people criticised that. It triggered a lot of self-doubt in me. Anyone who says it doesn't hurt at the start is lying.

'Girls Behind Bars' was the first film in the USA series, and it was the point at which I started to find my feet when it came to understanding what made a good TV documentary. People would disagree with that statement – and did – but for me it was a massive step forward.

It was focused around women in prison in the US; a hardcore topic in a country where more women are locked up than anywhere else in the world. I was going to spend time at two very different institutions to see how they compared. The first was Lakeview Shock Incarceration Correctional Facility, a military-style boot-camp prison in upstate New York, where the inmates go through a 'shock' programme aimed at rehabilitating them for the outside world. The second was Bayview Correctional Facility, a regular, medium-security prison in the unusual location of downtown New York, which housed women serving anything from three years to life.

I was feeling quite intimidated. There was so much I didn't know about the issues and problems faced by women in prison. And the characters I met were quite complicated. For some, being in prison was circumstantial – they were really decent girls who had found themselves in bad situations or been really unlucky: wrong place and time. Other girls were horrendous, violent murderers. What surprised me was who among them I did or didn't like – and how my beliefs changed during the making of the film.

It all began early one morning as I watched the newest intake of prisoners arrive at Lakeview in upstate New York. From the moment they stepped out of the prison van in handcuffs and leg irons, these women's lives were totally regimented, army-style. They were divided into platoons and drilled like soldiers, sticking to a super-strict timetable and obeying precise rules and regulations. It felt very American to me – very, 'Yes, Sir! No, Sir!' – and a bit over the top. No wonder it was called 'doing shock'. It looked totally traumatic, like something out of a nightmare.

Lakeview takes prisoners who are facing up to three years in a traditional prison for non-violent crimes, but choose to reduce their sentence to six months of shock. The aim of the Lakeview programme is to 'shock' inmates out of criminal behaviour by putting them through a military-style boot camp and to help them learn self-discipline and structure, so that on release they can get back on the right track and stay there. It's all about breaking negative thought and behaviour patterns, and some of the staff compare it to 'tough love'.

It's a voluntary programme that inmates choose to sign up to – and it's incredibly intensive and challenging, physically and emotionally. Nearly half of the women don't make it through to the end and are either sent to a traditional prison to serve a longer term or returned to court for resentencing. But the girls who do complete their six months in shock are less likely to reoffend for three years after their release than prisoners in regular prison, and generally less likely to end up in prison again. So something's working, but what?

On their arrival, the girls were given ugly green uniforms. Then they had their hair buzz cut to a quarter of an inch in length. Some of them had lovely long hair and tears streamed down their cheeks as it fell to the floor. I really felt for them – the haircuts seemed really symbolic to me, almost as if each inmate was being stripped of her individuality and girliness. But I was told that it was done for practical reasons, because they were only allowed three-minute showers.

'Tell me how to have a shower in three minutes?' I asked some of the girls as they were queuing up for the bathroom.

'Put your shampoo in your hair before you go in there,' one of them said, 'and rinse off real quick.'

She looked away. If you got caught talking in the queue, your shower time was reduced to one minute. Armpits and fanny, in and out.

Almost all of them were unhappy about it. 'I want a proper shower. I miss my hair. I'm devastated that I'm not allowed to wear makeup,' they told me.

But one girl said, 'I've never felt so comfortable. I'm not just gay for the stay, I am a gay woman. I feel much more comfortable with my hair shaved and wearing these conservative overalls.'

She hadn't felt she could dress to express her sexuality before – but in prison she could.

I spent time with the women who made up G1 platoon. Every morning, when the whistle blew, they had eight minutes to get up, get dressed, make their bed and tidy their locker. They did two hours of exercise before going to breakfast in the canteen, where they had to wait to be told to sit down. They needed permission to talk, wash, eat, go to the toilet, everything. They had eight minutes to eat their food. It was really tough. I don't think I would have lasted three minutes.

During breakfast on my first day, I noticed one of the newer inmates eating standing up. She told me it was her punishment for not sitting down properly. This was Tiffany; she was 23 and the first prisoner I got really pally with. Tiffany was really hard work. She wouldn't have anything to do with me for the first day or two. She wouldn't keep eye contact when we talked and she'd end up snarling at me.

I realised I would have to prove myself to her and the other girls if I was going to get them to open up. But it wasn't easy being this little white English girl surrounded by all these hard-ass women. I was so inexperienced, and they just weren't taking me seriously. So I had to be persistent.

I was *so* persistent.

I kept standing next to Tiffany and saying, 'You alright?'

She'd be like, 'Fuck off.'

'OK,' I'd say, as if I didn't take it to heart.

Then slowly she began to thaw.

I remember the moment I finally broke the ice. We were all sitting around a table and one of the girls turned to me and said, 'Didn't fancy doing your hair today?'

My hair was in a messy bun with bits falling out. Yes, it did look shit, but when it's dirty and you're working you just tie it back, don't you?

The other girls laughed.

It was just a bit of cheap point scoring and I thought, You cheeky bugger! I'm working hard here …

I don't know where it came from, but I said, 'You can fucking talk. You haven't got any hair. You've had all yours shaved off.'

The girls were like, 'Oh!'

I gulped. But actually, in hindsight, it's the best thing I could have done because it put us on more of a level playing field and we started getting on. It was the opening of the gate, I suppose. They thought, Oh, OK. She's got something about her.

Later on, I asked one of the girls, 'Where are you from?'

'Brooklyn,' she said. 'What do you know about Brooklyn?'

'Biggie Smalls is from Brooklyn,' I said.

Their eyebrows shot up. 'Oh, she knows about The Notorious!'

After that, we got really friendly, really quickly. I was there every day from before sunrise until lights out at 9.30pm and I think I was a welcome distraction. The girls' lives were so mundane, predictable and controlled that they enjoyed having this English idiot to play with. They weren't stupid – they realised that they wouldn't have to take part in the classes or the workouts when we were filming with them. So, the longer they sat talking to us, the more they'd be able to skive. It was a win–win situation on both sides.

As I got friendlier with Tiffany, I became a bit mesmerised by her. Since none of the inmates had any hair, you could only focus on their faces and Tiffany's face was incredibly striking. She was one of the most beautiful women I've seen. But she was frightening. She was an ex-gang member, an ex-Blood, who had been convicted on a gun charge. Out in the world, she'd spent her nights taking pills and selling drugs at a crack house. She made $2,000 a night and never managed to get home in time to wake up her daughter for school in the morning. She was lucky to have her mum to care for her daughter, especially while she was in prison. One of the big issues for female prisoners is anxiety about how their kids are coping without them.

Tiffany's problem was that she'd been addicted to her lifestyle – the money, drugs and guns.

'I was like a boy, always walking around with a gun,' she told me. 'It was a part of my outfit.' She made a face. 'Now I'm talking about guns my whole palm is itchy.'

'Cos you want the gun?' I asked.

'Yeah.'

'Would you ever use it?'

'If I had to.'

At one point she moved towards me and put her hand on my thigh. 'You know I like girls, isn't it?' she said.

Uh-oh, I thought.

But we became pals after we'd got over the fact that I wasn't gay – and she started telling me about her girlfriend and how she really struggled with jealousy.

I felt guilty about liking Tiffany. She had done these terrible things and yet I felt drawn to her. Every morning when I arrived at Lakeview I'd go and see her and find out how her night had been. It was quite confusing for me. I was very inexperienced and I was forming friendships with all these convicts who were in prison for really hardcore stuff.

The shock regime stripped them down and made them seem vulnerable at times, but I could never be sure how sincere they were being with me. When you're talking to me and you start crying, is it really you? I'd wonder. Is it a mask? Are you acting? Are you a real nightmare, or is it circumstantial that you're here?

Nothing is ever totally black or white so I'm sure it was a bit of both.

Another girl I got really friendly with was Sharon, who was inside for aggravated robbery – mugging people with guns, basically. She was properly scary. I could easily imagine her coming for me on the street. I kept thinking, If I was your victim you would frighten the life out of me!

When I first met Sharon, she was struggling to keep up on the pre-breakfast run. The next time I saw her, she was complaining about the whole group being punished because one person had broken a rule. Someone had gone to the bathroom when she shouldn't have, so everybody was having to run a lap of the dorm with their mattress on their head.

'We gotta pay for everybody else, which is un-freaking fair,' she grumbled.

'Can you see how some of the girls get frustrated because it's not them that did the wrong thing, yet they're still having to pay?' I said to the drill instructor in charge.

He explained that the group had to learn to hold each other accountable. He compared the situation to Sharon and her family.

'Think about the pain that your family feels every day that you're not home, where you belong,' he said to her. 'They did absolutely nothing but stick by you … Your family's paying for you every day.'

The staff constantly challenged the girls' thinking, trying to push them to a higher level of self-awareness. But they didn't seem to be getting very far with Sharon. So she was called up to the weekly disciplinary committee, where they addressed her 'negative body language' and gave her a 'positive attitude sash' to wear for a week as a constant reminder to improve her outlook.

It was a really embarrassing big yellow sash and I couldn't help taking the piss out of her. 'I don't really want to be seen dead with you in that sash,' I said.

'I know!' she replied. 'What can I do?'

'Tell me what your mates would say on the street if they saw you knocking about in it,' I asked.

'They'd say, "What the hell is wrong with you?"' she said, and admitted that she had wanted to cry when they gave it to her. 'But I refuse to cry,' she added. She was determined not to let anything break her down.

The platoon were encouraged to air their grievances with each other in group therapy sessions. The atmosphere in these sessions could be really intense and I felt uncomfortable at how hard the counsellors pushed the girls to open up about their life stories. Some of the stuff they'd experienced was horrendous.

In one of the sessions I attended, Sharon was in the firing line for her attitude and constant complaining. The other girls really laid into her.

'What's wrong with you … really? Tell your peers what's going on,' asked the counsellor leading the group.

Sharon finally broke down. Haltingly she explained that she had been hurt so many times in her life that her hostile attitude was a defence mechanism against being hurt again. Then she opened up about being sexually abused at the age of 12. She had tears just pouring down her face in front of all these weird, scary girls – and then loads of the girls started crying too.

Suddenly, the penny dropped.

Oh God, I thought. *I'm in a room full of girls who have had a really difficult time.*

It's shocking how many female prisoners have suffered violence from partners, sexual assault or childhood sexual abuse. When you know the figures, you can see that they're the product of their environment and the way they act is learned behaviour. After that, you can't help but warm to them and want what's best for them, even when they're scaring you.

The session didn't stop there. The counsellor kept pushing. His approach seemed too harsh and I felt uneasy. I didn't know where to look; I worried he was going too far. But then he pressed Sharon until she cracked and admitted she needed help from the rest of the girls to work on her attitude and behaviour. Until then, she had been defiant and unapproachable. It seemed like a real breakthrough.

'I need help and I want help and I would appreciate it if all of you would help me,' she said.

And every single one of them volunteered to help her.

After the session, I went over to Sharon and asked if I could talk to her. I felt worried for her and wanted to know how she felt about what had happened. But instead of being traumatised, she seemed relieved to have got things off her chest. 'I never thought I would say that to anybody I didn't know,' she told me. 'So for me to break down that wall, that felt good to me. It really did.'

She grabbed my hand. 'Stacey, you know, you've been such a pal to me and I just thank you so much,' she said.

It was really unexpected. I was so glad that I'd been able to help.

Like most of the girls in shock, Sharon was longing to taste freedom again. But I didn't see that same hunger in inmate Nicole Hartman, who seemed to keep sabotaging her chances of leaving Lakeview. Nicole was 22 and had been sentenced for drink driving with her young children in the car. She seemed desperate to see her kids, but would behave appallingly whenever her time neared the end. Then the staff would say, 'Well, we'll have to keep you back. You have to stay longer because you keep messing up.'

The shock programme lasts six months but inmates can be kept in longer if they don't seem ready to leave. It's called 'recycling' – and Nicole had been recycled twice during her ten months at Lakeview; the first time for anger issues, the second for fighting.

It made me wonder, Does she keep doing it because she's so frightened to go back out to the real world? Because she knows what's waiting for her?

I sat in on a group therapy session led by Counsellor Kubick, who ran the drug and alcohol programme at Lakeview. Counsellor Kubick told me that almost 75 per cent of Lakeview's inmates arrived with a history of addiction – a shocking number – and that the first part of the programme was aimed at detoxing them.

In the session, Nicole talked about her father, who was an established figure in a biker club, something like the Hells Angels. Nicole's upbringing had been really difficult. She'd seen a lot of violence and drug taking in her early life. When she was nine, both her parents had gone to prison. She went into foster care until she was 15. Then her mother got out of jail.

'I went and lived with her,' she said. 'I'd started drinking and smoking weed. I smoked weed and I drank with my mom. We used to go rob stuff together. She wasn't really a mom, per se.

'I met my husband. He was a drug dealer for my dad. He was selling drugs for my dad. I started selling a lot of drugs.'

Predictably, like so many of the girls at Lakeview, she'd found herself living a similar life to her parents. When her mum wasn't around, she stepped into her role in the family. She was her dad's right-hand man. She ran his errands; she 'took the heat for him' when needed.

'Family always comes first, no matter what,' she said solemnly.

It sounded like a message that had been drummed into her over and over again. And yet she had learned through her therapy sessions at Lakeview that her family relationships were dysfunctional and her mum and dad were probably best avoided. You could see she was torn between family loyalty and striking out alone to make a better, healthier life for herself.

Counsellor Kubick felt that Nicole had come a long way during her time at Lakeview, but seemed quite pessimistic about her chances when she got out. 'She's so far enmeshed into this family dysfunction that six months isn't going to take all of that away,' she said.

I felt really sorry for Nicole. I think you have to take responsibility for your own behaviour, your own choices and your own actions, but I also think you have to bear in mind the backgrounds a lot of these girls come from. It's hard to break out of learned patterns of behaviour and the opportunities aren't always there.

We took a break from Lakeview to visit a regular, medium-security prison for women in New York City. This was the type of prison where the girls who don't make it through shock go to serve out their original sentence. I was beginning to think that shock wasn't as bad as I'd originally thought because of the emphasis on therapy and rehabilitation – but which programme was better for getting the inmates back on the straight and narrow?

Bayview was a real eye opener. It was a high-rise prison in a crazy location, smack bang in the middle of Manhattan. I spent time in the eight-storey housing unit, on a floor that housed 37 women, some of them lifers.

It was very different to Lakeview. The girls become really unfit because they're just sitting around all day and they're not mentally stimulated. It wasn't easy finding an inmate who was willing to show me around, but eventually Danielle offered; she was serving a six-year sentence for badly injuring someone while drink driving. Danielle was incredible. She was the daughter of an alcoholic single mum and her upbringing sounded really chaotic. Her mother had taken heroin, smoked crack, snorted coke and got drunk for much of her childhood. Finally, she committed suicide. Danielle and a friend came home to find her dead in the living room. I can't imagine how horrendous that must have been. No wonder Danielle became an addict herself.

Amazingly, she went on to turn her life around at Bayview, spending her time there getting an education. She was planning to study for a degree when she got out.

'Before I came here, I was a waste of existence,' she said, 'and I'm not going to be that when I leave.'

First, she showed me the bathroom, where the girls went to hang out, or fight. 'If you want to be out of view, someone will lock the door, hold the door and block the window so no one can see, or you go in the shower area,' she said.

'How bad can it get?' I said, thinking I wouldn't last 30 seconds in there.

'Just fighting. I mean, nobody dies, if that's what you mean.'

'This is where we come if one of us is really horny,' another girl told me. 'We have mistresses and bitches. You're small, you've got red hair, so you would be a definite bitch. There's no way that you wouldn't do what the bigger girls were asking.'

A lot of them were 'gay for the stay' and had girlfriends they called wives, but on the outside they were straight and fancied men. It was just a circumstantial thing – if you're in there a long time, you're likely to want to get pleasured. Some of them were quite territorial over their wives and if they thought another girl was looking at their wife, that would be enough to start a fight. There were some proper scraps in there. The staff had to hide the cans of food because the girls used the lids to blade each other.

Every day in Bayview is the same for the inmates. You wake up, you argue, you kick off and you worry about not having enough money to buy what you need in the supplies store and then you fight because you're angry, you score and get fingered in the toilets.

It was depressing and draining and I couldn't get out of there fast enough.

After a couple of days at Bayview seeing how traditional prison works, we went back upstate to Lakeview, where the next wave of boot campers were graduating. Nicole was supposed to be among them, but she was stalling again. In the days before she was due to leave, she started back talking the staff and using hostile body language, sabotaging her chances of getting out. Eventually she told one of the staff that she was afraid of going home. She requested a session with Counsellor Kubick.

'It's scary, because everything that I left at home is at home waiting,' she said in the session. 'Just like I'm counting down days to go home, all my problems are counting down days until I can come back, so … it's scary.'

After ten months in shock, she recognised that her family relationships were toxic and had decided to live apart from her parents, but she was worried about where that left her. 'How am I going to do all the stuff that I need to do by myself?'

I was sad to see her mum and dad arrive to pick her up when it was time to leave. She automatically went with them; it was like waving her off to the lion's den. It's hard for most of these women to rehabilitate and then keep straight, but with parents like hers, I felt it was going to be even more difficult.

As it turned out, Nicole was right to be scared. Within a week of leaving Lakeview she was involved in another drink-driving incident with her kids. This time she lost an arm. It was tragic and horribly inevitable. It was just too hard for her to break out of the environment she was familiar with, even knowing how damaging it was for her.

Does prison ever really work? I think we could probably find a better way of helping the people who find themselves in the system. In fact, it sometimes feels like we've totally lost sight of what prison is actually for. Of course it's for punishment and it's supposed to act as a deterrent, but shouldn't it also be helping people who find it hard to function legally in society, for whatever reason?

If you asked me which was the better prison system out of the two I saw, I would definitely say the Lakeview boot camp. I wasn't expecting to come to that conclusion because Lakeview's shock programme felt so over the top at first. But there seemed to be real commitment among the staff to get results – and they really did seem to believe that these girls deserved a second chance. There was more momentum and purpose at Lakeview than at the regular prison, where I had the feeling that you're sometimes left to rot. There was no sense of urgency when it came to genuine rehabilitation at Bayview, although obviously Danielle's was an exceptional story.

Making this programme, I realised that a massive number of girls and women in prison in the US have grown up in chaotic households, been abused and have a history of mental illness and substance abuse. So many of them are a product of their environment and the traumas they have experienced. The boot-camp programme tried to address that and shake things up for them, so they could start again. The regular prison did far less of that. It was just somewhere to dump people who were being punished. Like a lot of people, I'd like to see a lot more resources put into education, training and counselling in prison, to give people more of a chance when they're outside again.

I was really proud of 'Girls Behind Bars' when it was finished. Even though at times I felt out of my depth in the situations I was in, I felt it was a strong documentary because we had amazing access to the prisons and tackled the subject head on. Oh, and it was the first time I'd done my own commentary.

It was pretty well received, but some critics couldn't help slamming aspects of my presentation style. Some of it was fair enough, but sometimes it felt a bit irrelevant. It would often be middle-aged, middle-class male critics, saying, 'Once you get past her accent … ' or, 'She's like a caricature,' or, 'She dresses a lot younger than her years.' The fact that I used to work in a perfume shop at Luton Airport was mentioned in almost every review. Nonsense like that; stuff that didn't even matter.

The thing is, when people are rinsing you and poking fun at your accent and style, there is a temptation to conform. I was so gutted about what they were saying that I started thinking, Oh God, they all hate me, and they're right! What am I doing? If I start talking in a different way, perhaps they will take me seriously.

I'm so, so pleased that I didn't cave in to the pressure or that temptation, because I would have been pretending to be something that I've never been, and have no interest in being. And, whatever you do for a living, it takes time to perfect your role, right?

Still, it took me a long time to get used to being criticised. I'm totally confident about who I am and what I do now, but that self-assurance comes with age and confidence, I think. Back then I was so, so mortified and devastated by it.

It wasn't just the professionals. Viewers were also leaving comments like, 'It's such a bad example to the youth of today that you can stumble your way into a TV career with no learning, effort or ability. It makes me feel truly sorry that I pay my TV licence.'

It makes me smile to read that now, but I was too full of self-doubt at the time to see the funny side. The worst thing I read was a tweet from someone saying, 'I hope you die.'

I read lovely things as well, but didn't really entertain them. I focused specifically on the nasty, negative stuff, and felt totally confused as to why people were being so unkind. *Oh God, this is awful and horrific!* I thought.

At that age, it's easy to place a lot of importance on somebody else's opinion of you. You instantly think you have to alter yourself. Now, though – honestly, with my hand on my heart – I could not care less. I used to give the critics lots of time, but now the only opinions I listen to come from people I rate, or I've met and think are awesome. If someone I respect says something critical, I'll take it on board and say, 'Yes, OK.' But if it's somebody I've not even met, I just think, *Oh, who cares?*

With age, I've realised that the critics are well within their rights to say what they like. They're entitled to their opinions; they've got a job to do. You're not going to be everyone's cup of tea. Some people will really get you, admire you, and like you, and other people will not be able to understand why you've been given the gig. That's fine. I just leave them to it.

Obviously, I disagree with a lot of what they say. I think it's predictable that they want to continue seeing the same traditional journalism that we've had for the last 50 years. They can't see that the very reason I've been given the gig is because I'm different.

As for the trolling on social media, you can't help seeing and reading the nasty stuff; it's in your face. I just feel sorry for the trolls though, because I think they're sad lunatics, sat in their bedrooms, having a wank, keyboarding.

This may sound cheesy, but it's totally true: you just have to stick to who you are, and deliver what you believe. There's always compromise when you're making documentaries, but you have to feel like you and your subject have been fairly represented. And the first time I truly had that sense was when I watched the final edit of 'Girls Behind Bars'.

2

Maria

Immigration

The first time I saw a dead body was in Mexico in 2012. It caught me off guard. I really struggled with it and for a few weeks I couldn't get it out of my mind.

It was the body of a young woman. She had beautiful black curly hair. I kept seeing her when I closed my eyes, kept remembering the smallest details. There was a hairband beside her, with strands of her hair still in it. She was carrying an ID card and a couple of pesos – a tiny amount of money, perhaps enough for a can of coke. Apart from that, she had nothing, except for the clothes she was wearing.

Like thousands before her, she had died of thirst in the Sonoran Desert trying to reach a better life in the US. Her body was already decomposing when the Border Patrol found her. I'll never forget that smell. It was horrendous, like burning.

It was my first time in Mexico and I was at the US border with a film crew to make a programme about the hundreds of thousands of migrants who try to slip unseen into America every year. Many of them travel thousands of miles up the continent from South and Central America. They pay people smugglers – known as 'coyotes' – to guide them across the desert.

This last stage of their journey is the deadliest: walking for up to five days in the suffocating heat across the dry desert with barely enough water to keep them alive. Many of them get caught and sent back. Others die of thirst, exhaustion or snakebites. Some get raped or robbed on the way. And a whole load make it across to Arizona and on to California and other US states, where the American Dream awaits – or at least a fruit-picking job that pays enough to send money to their struggling families back home.

Staring out across the desert at the Mexican border in the blazing heat, I wondered just how bad things had to be at home to risk your life walking for days and nights across such a wilderness. The day was so, so hot – heat like I'd never felt before – but at night the temperature drops and it gets really, really cold. I tried to imagine what it would be like. You'd just walk and walk and walk, because you've got to get there, and all the while you know there are people out there trying to catch you: choppers in the air, patrol cars on both sides. You have to be so desperate and determined to make it.

Not in a million years could I see myself managing it, but it's estimated that just over 11 million undocumented migrants have found a way into the US unseen. Around half of them are Mexican, with two million at least fleeing poverty and violence in countries like Honduras and Guatemala. Their journey is difficult and dangerous, but it's more than worth it if they make it. They feel there's nothing for them back home; over the border lies a living and a future.

It wasn't easy to film on the Mexican border. The border towns are controlled by brutal cartels who are at war with each other and don't like having strangers on their patch. The news was full of reports of mass killings and headless bodies found by the roadside. It was definitely the most daunting place I had ever been to up till then.

Our way in was through a local priest called Padre Prisciliano, who had a unique relationship with the organised crime cartels. The Padre baptised everyone's kids in the area – whichever side they were on – and managed to help the migrants without antagonising the gang members. I think they let him get on with it because they're so scared of God. It was really weird – they killed people Monday to Saturday and then went to church on Sunday and hung off the Padre's every word.

He hated what they did, but carried on with his job as best he could in a place where people went around killing other people in everyday life. That was just the way it was. It wasn't normal but it was normalised. The Padre knew the rules and who not to piss off.

He was so respected that he was able to bring in the occasional film crew without anyone getting murdered – as long as they obeyed the rules. A couple of weeks before we arrived, he'd had a French news crew with him.

'Don't wander off,' he warned them. 'Wherever I go, you go. Just stick with me.'

'Yeah, yeah, yeah,' they'd agreed. Then, shock horror, they wandered off.

A couple of hours later, he got a phone call from a cartel member.

'We've got a couple of French individuals here and they're saying they're with you. Are they? If they're not, we're going to kill them.'

'Don't kill them! They're with me,' he yelled.

He had to drop everything and rush out to collect these French journalists. When he arrived, they were hanging upside down, naked. The cartel member apologised to him and untied them.

'I told you not to wander off! This is not a joke; this is a hostile environment,' he berated them.

When I heard this story, I was stunned by the scale of what was going on and how real it was on the ground. The Padre was just about the only guy that the cartel members didn't want to annoy, so I stuck to him like glue wherever he went. Without his blessing, we couldn't have made the film. He gave us the most amazing access. But I felt super nervous when he wasn't around, especially after I found out that he'd told everyone we were missionaries.

One day when I was back in my hotel and the Padre was elsewhere, I heard someone whistling in the empty, echoey corridor outside my room. I was feeling so edgy that it sounded really sinister. Was it a secret signal? To a masked assassin? My skin crawled with fear. Was the door to my room going to fly open any second with a burst of semi-automatic gunfire?

It turned out to be nothing, just a guy whistling – but it really had me going for a moment. It was a really scary place.

I wanted to meet some of the migrants preparing to cross the desert, so the Padre took me to Altar, a border town where migrants picked up their final bits and bobs before they set out – water bottles and clothes, that sort of thing. He knew the managers of a ramshackle hostel and felt it would be safe for me to speak to some of the people staying there.

The hostel was used by migrants to rest or sleep before they began the 60-mile crossing. No one wanted to hang around long, though. The rooms were dingy and airless and strewn with discarded belongings; the migrants slept three to a bed and often emptied out their backpacks to make room for provisions and water before they left. There was so much they had to take with them, including jumpers for the freezing night, which they had to carry throughout the blazing hot day, when they were roasting.

There was a weird tension in the air at the hostel because everyone was waiting for the moment their coyote would show up to say it was time to set out across the border. Some of them had been waiting a week, gearing themselves up mentally and physically for the challenge that lay ahead – and you could sense the frustration building up inside them. But when I met Maria, who was hoping to leave the following day, she seemed quite relaxed. Maria was such a sweetheart. She was only 19, ridiculously young to be so far from home, alone and unprotected.

'You seem older!' I said.

She grinned. She had a smile that could light up a room. 'That's because I've lived my life in advance,' she said.

She spoke lightly, but you could tell that she'd had a tough time. She had grown up in Oaxaca, one of the poorest states in Mexico, where a lot of the population live at the most basic level of subsistence. She had two children and one of them was disabled; her mum was looking after them while she made the long journey north. I could tell how hard it had been for her to leave them behind. She hadn't brought any photos because she didn't want to have to throw them away to make room in her backpack.

'I'm carrying their images in my head and heart,' she said, her eyes shining with emotion.

Maria had paid a coyote to bring her the 2,000 miles from her hometown to Altar. Now she was paying another coyote to take her across the border and up to LA. It was costing her $7,000. She had no pals with her; she was totally alone. She was there out of pure desperation.

'When I was at school, I swear I never thought I'd end up here,' she told me. 'I could never have imagined that I'd leave my hometown.'

She seemed upbeat about the journey that lay ahead, though. 'The thing is, you have to be positive and not let yourself be beaten,' she said. 'Right now I'm safe and calm because my two children are alright. Everything depends on me. If I get worried, nervous or afraid, it doesn't do any good.'

She definitely had the right attitude – but I wondered how easy it was to stay calm when you were heading out into the unknown like that. Then I noticed that she only had one water bottle with her. For five days walking? She said it would be enough, but I felt worried for her.

She lit a candle as she was leaving. 'So that God will light our path and help us through,' she explained. She promised to send me a message through Facebook if she made it to the other side.

Something told me Maria would be successful. I'm going to see her on the other side, I thought. Why not her? After all, a lot of people make it.

I would have loved to get more of an insight into what it was like for her to attempt the crossing, but in the end we decided against giving her a handycam to take with her. The journey was treacherous enough. We didn't want to expose her to extra risk.

The Padre blessed each group of migrants as they set out. I asked him what he thought Maria's chances were of getting to America.

'Maria is really strong and determined,' he said. 'But she will probably have trouble with people she comes across who will want to abuse her. Because she's young. Because she has a nice body.'

Some of the coyotes were known to behave fairly decently, in that they didn't take advantage of the migrants sexually or exploit them financially. It was a straight transaction: You give me the money; I'll take you across. Others were just there to kick these people when they were down and exploit them at their most vulnerable time, which was horrendous.

'But we can't tell her, "Don't go,"' said the Padre, 'because she's going to say, "Well, feed and clothe me then."'

This summed it up for me: if people could earn a halfway decent living at home then they wouldn't be willing to jeopardise everything for a better life in the US. Maria wasn't doing it out of greed. She just wanted to be able to make enough to support her family and give her kids a better future. She couldn't do that at home in Oaxaca. Otherwise she would have stayed. Trying to cross the border is often a completely desperate act. The fact that more than 175,000 unaccompanied kids from Central America were rounded up by the US

Border Patrol in the five years between 2011 and 2016 says a lot, I think.

Like Maria, most of the mothers I met on the border had left their kids with family members and hoped to send for them when they were settled in the US. But Manuela, who was stranded in Altar with her little boy, Pedro, hadn't found it in her heart to leave her son behind.

I met Manuela, Pedro and their family friend, Jorge, through the Padre. They were in dire straits after agreeing to pay a coyote $6,000 to take them from Guatemala to Los Angeles. The trip was supposed to take 15 days, but when they ran out of money their coyote abandoned them at the border, where they had been stuck for three months. It was a horrible place to be, a no man's land, a limbo.

They were thinking of attempting the crossing anyway, but now Manuela was worried that little Pedro was too ill to make the journey. In desperation, she had turned to the priest for help. The Padre sent her to a Red Cross mobile unit, where Pedro was treated for his cough and fever. One of the medical staff gave her a leaflet full of advice for people crossing the border, including a list of things to take: water, salt, matches, lemons, tinned food, high-legged footwear and garlic, which is a natural snake repellent.

'Right now we don't have those things,' Jorge said.

The leaflet brought home the potential dangers of the trip and I felt like pleading with them not to risk it. I was worried about Manuela's chances because she was planning to carry little Pedro all that way. He was only three and there was no way he could walk it by himself, but although Manuela was strong and sturdy, carrying that extra weight would make the trek twice as hard.

Some of the tales I'd heard about the crossing were really shocking: of people being raped and battered on the way; others feverishly begging passersby for a sip of water as they slowly died of thirst; dead bodies under trees; human bones lying out in the sun; migrants who had been abandoned by their coyote walking round and round in circles, lost and disorientated, until they collapsed. It sounded surreally bad.

Girls and young women were especially vulnerable; it was very easy for the coyotes to take advantage of them as they led them across the border, because they didn't have a leg to stand on legally. The authorities weren't going to listen if you said you were gang raped while you were crossing the desert – because you shouldn't have been there in the first place.

I think the US Border Patrol saw the migrants more as numbers than people, anyway. There wasn't much sympathy there. They called them 'illegal aliens', which made them sound like they weren't even human. It was funny how the labels varied among the people I spoke to – people more sympathetic to their cause called them 'undocumented migrants'; to others they were aliens and criminals.

Trump criticised Mexicans throughout his election campaign. In his presidential announcement speech, he said of Mexican migrants: 'They're bringing drugs; they're bringing crime; they're rapists; and some, I assume, are good people.'

I asked several people, from the Padre and the hostel owners to the Border Patrol guys, if any of the migrants were caught with drugs. They all said no. Drug smuggling was a separate issue altogether.

'There's a right way to cross into America and there's a wrong way,' the Border Patrol guys told me. 'These people are taking the wrong way and we need to lock them up.'

It was very straightforward to them. The migrants were breaking the law and their job was to catch as many of them as possible. It was cat-and-mouse, a numbers game, and they seemed delighted every time they closed in on someone.

I went up in a chopper on patrol with them. The size of the desert took my breath away. It was all I could see from the sky – desert stretching endlessly into the distance. I couldn't imagine anyone being able to walk from one end to the other. It seemed too enormous. I would cry if someone asked me to walk across it. My knees would buckle. I just couldn't do it.

Eventually, we swooped down and landed about two miles from the border, at a place called Horse Peak. There was a small group of migrants battling their way across the desert, including a young woman who was seven months pregnant. She had carpet wrapped around her feet so that she didn't leave footprints in the sand and when she saw the helicopter, she started running, stumbled and fell. I felt so worried for her as she lay on the ground clutching her stomach, crying in pain and frustration. It was awful. She was Guatemalan and had come such a long way.

The Border Patrol guys said that a lot of women try to cross the border when they're pregnant so that they can have their babies in America – they call them 'anchor babies' because the child automatically qualifies for US citizenship and can go on to sponsor other members of the family when it becomes an adult. A lot of people in the US see it as a cynical, uncaring move by a mum-to-be to try to get into America while pregnant, but this girl looked so ragged and weary that my heart went out to her. The fact that she was prepared to risk her own health and that of her baby to get to a better life did not seem cynical or callous. It was an act of desperation. And it had failed.

So many of the migrants I spoke to said that they weren't looking for an easy life. They just wanted to survive and earn a living wage. Back home in Guatemala, Manuela's friend Jorge had worked his socks off from five in the morning until eleven at night as an apprentice tailor, earning just $5 a day. It just wasn't enough to live on. All he wanted was a job that paid the bills, away from the violence of the cartels. This was something I heard again and again. People would much rather be living a harder life on the other side than endure their previous existence, where they constantly felt their family were going to get killed or they were going to get shot or dragged into some kind of drug war. They just wanted the chance to earn a decent living in peace.

Imagine if England was a really poor country where you couldn't earn a living wage, where it was too dangerous to leave the house because of the drugs wars on the streets, and your kids were constantly under threat. Then imagine that Scotland was thriving and booming and it was safe to bring your kids up there. Of course we would all try and get into Scotland. There is just no way I wouldn't. You'd want to better yourself, better your kids, better your own life. I don't know how you can begrudge someone that – I just don't get it. I know borders are necessary and immigration has to be controlled; I know you can't let everyone in. But I think the way in which we deal with these individuals is sometimes so inhumane.

I don't know what the answer is, but people can't go on dying in their thousands trying to get into America. The dead girl I saw in the mortuary only wanted a job, like Maria. Maybe she had children, too – most of the women I met in Altar were risking everything because they wanted a better life for their children. I hate to think of how much she must have suffered out there in the desert. She died an excruciating death.

The ironic thing is that if all the illegal migrants in the US left the country, parts of America would probably grind to a halt without all the workers who keep the wheels turning, often doing the lowest paid jobs. Their contribution to the economy of states like California and Texas in tax revenues alone (including sales tax and tax on renting property) is reckoned to far exceed the cost of the services they use. That's why it's so unbelievable that Trump gathered the momentum to become president on a declaration that he would build a wall along the border to keep migrants out. Still, it was a vote winner.

At the other end of the spectrum are those who believe in a world with no borders. I don't think that's realistic either, because global inequality would drive millions of migrants to the US, Canada and other rich countries. Somehow there has to be a compromise, though.

Ideally, people would be able to stay in their own home towns and live and prosper if they chose to. If they can't do that, perhaps other countries should help to find an alternative for them. Either way, they shouldn't find themselves dying of thirst in the desert trying to reach a place where they can pick fruit for a halfway decent wage. Who are the ones who need protection here? Isn't it partly up to the US to protect these people against dying in their thousands?

There is also a complicated and heartbreaking human rights debate around deporting undocumented migrants. Life in the US has always been insecure for them, especially if they are black or noticeably Latino. If a police officer asks you for ID and you don't have it, you'll be arrested on the spot and sent home.

I heard some really sad stories – one mum I met had been packed off to Mexico in an instant after nearly two decades living in America, leaving her home and four children behind. I also met a guy who had been deported five times – he was trying to bust the border for a sixth time. One minute you're in the Land of the Free, the next minute you're gone. It's like an alien abduction – only it's the aliens being abducted.

When Trump became president, he vowed to prioritise the deportation of America's 11 million undocumented people, build a wall and all the rest of it. He also pledged to outlaw all the kids without papers who had arrived in the US as children. To many people, this was beyond unfair, because these kids had never chosen to go to the US in the first place, but had grown up and gone to school there. They were American in all but name, right?

The Obama administration wanted to offer legal residency to kids of illegal migrants who had grown up in the US under the bipartisan Development, Relief, and Education for Alien Minors (DREAM) Act – and the kids were nicknamed 'Dreamers'. But the measure was voted down and Obama ended up having to compromise with DACA (Deferred Action for Childhood Arrivals), an immigration policy put in place in 2012 to protect the children of undocumented parents.

To qualify for DACA, you had to have arrived in the country before the age of 16 and been under 31 in 2012. If you also passed vetting for criminal behaviour and security risk, you were eligible for a temporary visa that allowed you to live, work and study in the US for two years, after which you could apply to renew for another two years. It was a bit like living in a grey area between legal and illegal, but it was better than nothing.

Around 700,000 Dreamers had been granted approval when Trump decided to wind down DACA. His plan was to close the channel for new applications and end legal status for everyone else on the programme when their visas expired in 2020. What would happen then? Would people now in their twenties and thirties who were perhaps doctors, nurses, lawyers or teachers be sent 'home' to their country of origin – a country they weren't necessarily familiar with and may never even have visited? Did Trump care?

On the day he announced the end of DACA, Trump said, 'I have advised the department of homeland security that DACA recipients are not enforcement priorities unless they are criminals, are involved in criminal activity, or are members of a gang.'

In other words, the Dreamers wouldn't be top of the deportation list, but they would still be illegal aliens and could still be deported. At any time.

The decision to scrap DACA was immediately challenged and 15 states announced they were bringing lawsuits against the Trump administration. Then it looked like Trump might strike a deal with leading Democrats to allow the Dreamers to stay, as long as Congress agreed to measures to get tougher on immigration. Everyone was very specific about not including the border wall in the talks, though. The wall was not on the table, OK?

A month later Trump backtracked and issued a list of demands. He said Dreamers could stay only if Congress funded the wall, among other things (a non-starter for the Democrats). And so it rumbled on, leaving hundreds of thousands of young people feeling totally vulnerable, clinging on to the so-called American Dream by the skin of their teeth.

One of Trump's other demands was for a points-based immigration test, based on the Australian system, which wouldn't work in favour of people like Maria – or Jorge, Manuela and little Pedro – fleeing extreme poverty. If you interview people at the border then you're making choices and you're most likely going to choose middle-class, educated or skilled migrants. But the people living in poverty are still going to try and get across. Maybe the places people want to get to should make more of an effort to process their claims and welcome them in.

In the meantime, I think if you've walked through that desert and you've got to the other side successfully, you can only be an asset to the country that you arrive in, because the journey requires such determination, power and strength.

If someone can make that crossing, surely they can do a job that perhaps an American doesn't want to do. They are survivors.

I was so relieved when Maria contacted me on Facebook to say she'd made it to California. She was picking strawberries and being paid in a fortnight what it would have taken four months to earn at home.

I wanted to meet up with her, but we had to be careful that we weren't seen together. This was her life and it would be terrible for us to swoop in, film, get everything that we need to make a really interesting documentary, then leave and go back to our lives in England, only for Maria to have to deal with a knock on the door.

'Where do you want to meet?' I asked her. 'Where do you feel comfy? Tell me what you want to say; tell me what you don't. I just want to show what's really going on.'

She agreed to meet in a park near where she was staying. It was amazing to see her. She was wearing makeup, her hair was shining and she had a radiant expression on her face; she looked totally different from the dusty migrant I had met in Altar. Granted, her work conditions weren't probably great and people could still take advantage of her, but she was in a much, much better position than she had been a couple of weeks before – and it showed. Her horror story had ended. She could send money back to her mum and kids.

I asked her about the desert crossing: how difficult was it?

Her expression grew serious. 'You're really scared that you can get caught any time and sent back,' she said, shivering at the memory. 'It was really cold at night. I was very thirsty, very hungry and my feet were really hurting, but I never said, "I can't make it."'

Back home in Oaxaca, she was used to hardship. She was used to being hungry and driving herself physically. Her life had toughened her up for the crossing and made her determined to get across for her kids.

And yet there would always be the fear of being deported. 'At any moment you can be caught off guard and sent back to Mexico,' she said. She just had to live with it.

In 2012, about 300,000 people were caught at the border and deported to Mexico. In 2016, it was 400,000. The numbers will keep going up while there is this massive inequality between North and Central America. And, unless the US government takes a more humane approach to immigration, people from Mexico, Honduras and Guatemala will continue to die in the harsh Sonoran desert, trying to escape a life that isn't worth living.

3

Eva

Drugs

I had a definite set of opinions about drugs when I went to Peru in 2013. I was very conservative in my thinking; perhaps I was too simplistic.

I thought: Drugs ruin lives, therefore drugs are bad; we shouldn't be pro-drugs in any way.

Then I heard Eva's story and realised that, even with drugs, things aren't always black and white.

Five years earlier, a band of Colombian drug traffickers had crossed the border into north-eastern Peru. They travelled by boat along the river to Cushillo Cocha, a remote town on the banks of the Amazon. When they arrived, they gave the people an offer they couldn't refuse. *Grow coca leaves for us and we will pay you well.*

The inhabitants of Cushillo Cocha were living a hand-to-mouth existence, barely making enough from selling the crops they grew to feed themselves and their community. They saw the Colombian offer as a chance to step up out of poverty. But one woman refused to go along with it: Eva, a mother of five children, who was one of the town leaders. Eva was concerned that the coca leaf is the key ingredient in the manufacture of cocaine.

'As someone in authority, I couldn't do it, because you have to set a good example,' she told me.

It was a dilemma that people in the mountain regions of Peru, Bolivia and Colombia had often faced: Is it immoral to collaborate with the drugs cartels? Is it madness, considering their reputation for violence? Do you take their money and hope for the best?

Do you even have a choice?

Coca traditionally thrives on the lower slopes and highlands of the Andes, which is where nearly all the world's coca plants used to be cultivated. But when the US developed glyphosate chemicals that could zap and kill coca plants – and started crop spraying from planes as part of a massive programme of aerial eradication 20 years ago – they wiped out more than half of Colombia's coca crops. The cocaine cartels had to think again.

Nobody knows who developed Boliviana negra, also known as *supercoca* and *la millionaria*. No one is even sure if it was genetically modified in a lab or created by coca farmers crossbreeding different strains of plants. Either way, around the early 2000s, the Colombian cartels hit on a new variety of coca leaf that is both resistant to glyphosate and can be grown in the soggy lowlands of the Amazon basin. It's a super hardy plant that grows to double the size of its mountain cousin and yields a crop several times a year. Most importantly, it has the high alkaloid content required to make premium grade cocaine.

Bingo. The cartels immediately went one step ahead of the Americans, who've spent billions of US taxpayers' money trying to eradicate cocaine production in South America. It was the latest episode in the US war on drugs – and no one had a clue what would happen next.

As someone who had never taken drugs or had a real interest in drugs, I learned a massive amount in Peru, which in 2013 had just taken the title of world's biggest cocaine producer off Colombia. I went there to see what effect the arrival of *supercoca* was having on the communities that had been persuaded to grow it. So, while I was working on a series investigating the new frontlines of the global war on drugs – including new trafficking routes, new means of production and brand new drugs – I travelled to Cushillo Cocha to find out.

As I made my way down the Amazon in a wooden longboat, I passed clusters of tumbledown shacks on the riverbank where people appeared to be living very basic lives. Barely connected to the outside world, they were grindingly poor and kept out the tropical rains with roofs made from leaves.

Cushillo Cocha looked and felt very different from these communities, though. As my boat pulled up at the town's wharf, I noticed several houses with brick walls and tin roofs; some of them even had satellite dishes. It was a massive contrast. You could instantly see that there was money around, and the infrastructure felt much more solid.

The town's prosperity had made an incredible difference to people's lives. 'Growing coca, we've been able to make home improvements,' one man told me. 'We've bought a tin roof, a fan, a TV, mobile phones and a fridge where we can put meat, fish and fruit. We've been able to have cold water.'

He was 50 years old before he tried cold water, he explained. 'For me it's a joy.'

I could see why his face lit up at the thought of a cool drink. Sometimes it gets really, really hot in Cushillo Cocha.

As for Eva, she held tight to her principles when she saw her neighbours buying fridges and TVs. She and her husband Shuca refused to grow coca for five years. But when other mums came home from town with books and school equipment for their kids, she cracked.

'I've changed my mind about coca due to the needs of the family,' she told me. 'We have five children – two are adopted – and they need things. Since growing coca, we have been able to buy school equipment and clothes.'

Eva was a really lovely woman and it was the best of reasons. 'The kids deserve an education,' she added. 'They are our future.'

I saw a similar situation in Swaziland in Africa two years later, where I met a widowed grandmother who was growing and selling cannabis to support her family. With the money earned from her super-strong weed crop, this old lady was able to buy food and clothing for her grandkids and pay their school fees. In a country where HIV/AIDS and tuberculosis have decimated the population – and life expectancy is around 50 years old – she was determined to give the youngsters more security in the future.

But the difference between Swaziland and Peru was the risk factor. The farmer in charge of the Swazi granny's cannabis crop explained that there would only be minor repercussions if the authorities discovered their plants. Equally, the police don't have much of an official presence or function in the Amazonian swamps, either. But whereas a grower can sell his crop at the local market in Swaziland, the people of Cushillo Cocha in Peru are governed by the whims of Colombian narco-traffickers. And you'd have to be living in a bunker if you didn't know what kind of danger that can spell.

One of Cushillo Cocha's town leaders talked to me about the dangers of growing coca. 'We know it brings lots of problems and violence but we are thankful for these crops, because we can meet our needs and escape poverty,' he said.

It was quite an eye opener for me hearing this. I was anti-drugs and yet I could see how these really lovely families were benefiting from growing coca. Eva's dilemma was clear: she had these beautiful kids and all she wanted was for them to survive and flourish and become their own little characters. But they weren't able to do that unless they had the extra money from the coca, which gave them £600 a year, a massive amount of cash for a family that had been surviving on next to nothing. Hers was a hard decision ultimately. I admire her for holding out for so long but it's also totally understandable that she thought, If I do this, my kids might be able to leave and then go on to prosper elsewhere.

Like a lot of the topics I've covered over the years, the drugs issue as a whole struck me as contradictory and confusing. You think one thing one hour and the total opposite the next. So while I was spending time with Eva and her family and hearing about her kids getting school bags for the first time, I could see the positives. But the following day I had a conversation with a family in the next village along the river who had a totally different perspective.

When a gang of Colombian narcos realised that the conditions in the village were ideal for growing *supercoca*, they didn't give the villagers a choice about growing it on their land.

It wasn't, 'Do you want to become involved?' It was, 'You are going to be involved. We are going to use your land. You will do whatever we say and if you don't we will kill you.'

Suddenly my view shifted. These weren't Colombian nice guys bringing prosperity to a struggling community. The local priest told me that when six young men from the village raised objections to their plans, they tied them to a tree and set them on fire. It just shows that wherever there is an opportunity to benefit, there is also an opportunity to exploit and take advantage of the most vulnerable. That's what was happening there.

I felt worried for the people of Cushillo Cocha, because it was clear that you're not in charge when you're involved with drugs cartels. You have to take it as it comes. You grin and bear it, you play the game and ride the wave – but ultimately the people in control determine what's going to happen.

It was OK for Eva to refuse to play ball because there were already enough people in her village who were prepared to cooperate. The narcos had won over the entire space. They didn't need to win over just one family.

It's not just the poverty that is the problem. The whole area is so isolated and lawless, it's scary. We had to get a boat back and forth from the mainland to the locations where we were shooting, which meant a lot of trips up and down the river. I was on constant alert because we had been warned about a pirate who was going around robbing people; we were obvious targets because we had loads of expensive gear with us.

People kept saying, 'Whatever you do, don't get on that boat after six, when it's dark.'

Then of course our shoot overran one day and it was pitch black by the time we got on the boat. I was really worried that we'd set off so late. 'This is exactly what we were told not to do,' I kept saying nervously.

Thankfully, Stas, the cameraman on the shoot, is a good friend – he did his best to reassure me and I started to calm down. We're in the middle of the Amazon, I thought. The pirate is probably miles away. I'm sure we'll be fine if we're quick. So I lay on the deck and looked up at the sky. The stars were so beautiful that I zenned out a bit and forgot my panic about the pirate. This is unbelievable, I thought. I'm on a boat going down the Amazon River!

All of sudden I heard a massive bang. The boat rocked and shook, and suddenly I remembered where I was. Just get us back to land, I thought. Please! In fact, we had hit a gigantic log that was floating down the river. Thankfully the log split, rather than the boat, but we were all as terrified as each other. 'What's going on? Oh my God, it's the pirate.'

The two-week shoot involved constant travel in areas where getting from A to B was often a real struggle. If we weren't on a boat worrying about being attacked by a pirate, we were driving through the night for 11 hours, and eating ration packs because there was no food, and filming the moment we arrived. Or flying in planes that were so flimsy they were like paper planes, and so weighed down with our gear that I'd be thinking, This plane is going to crash! We're going to die! It was just very real, the Peru shoot, and very hard.

Early on in the shoot, in the VRAE, also known as 'cocaine valley' because it produces more coca than anywhere else on the planet, I went up into the San José hills on a mule called Charlie (yes, really). When I reached the plateau and looked down across the vast natural gorge, I could not believe my eyes. There was coca everywhere I looked, stretching for miles and miles and miles. It was a sea of coca, totally mind blowing. I'd been having trouble getting my head around the fact that the global cocaine retail market was worth $88 billion. Seeing those fields of coca brought home to me how huge the demand really was.

I wanted to see cocaine production at the next stage, so I went into the jungle near Santa Rosa to see it being made. It was a really tense trip because outsiders weren't welcome in Santa Rosa, which was notorious for producing vast quantities of cocaine. Our contact was a total sweetheart, but he was completely paranoid about getting caught by someone from the cartel and his fear was contagious. I was pretty wound up by the time we arrived at the cocaine laboratory, which was surrounded by thick forest.

'Cocaine laboratory' makes it sound like it should be full of sophisticated equipment, but it was a makeshift operation using plastic sheeting, tubs, buckets, wellies, rubber gloves and garden hoses. This was where a great mulch of leaves was being made into coca paste, which would later be purified to produce a coca base and then converted into cocaine powder.

When I asked the guy who was extracting coke from the leaves how he felt about the impact of coke on the people who took it, he said that he thought cocaine's main purpose was to give soldiers courage when they went into war. He'd being doing the job for 14 years but seemed to have no idea about the wider implications of the drug trade. Having seen people get addicted to coke at home, and having seen their lives destroyed by it, I was shocked by his innocence.

Under a canvas shelter there was an ancient microwave oven that looked like it might explode at any moment – Health & Safety would have had a fit just at the sight of it. While one of the cooks was heating up a bunch of coke inside it, I noticed our fixer starting to look a bit spaced. This is very odd, I thought.

When the coke was cooked, he and the others started saying, 'Please try some. It's so pure. You've come all this way and you're going to miss out.'

That's the last thing I need! I thought. The absolute last thing I need right now – in this circus, in this calamity – is a line of gear. It's literally so far down on my list.

I will take a sandwich, though, because I'm totally ravenous ...

*

I think people find it hard to believe that I've never had any interest in taking drugs. It wasn't as if I'd lived a sheltered life: drugs were always available when I was growing up in Luton. My pals did loads of gear. Everyone was taking pills and sniffing coke. Boys would take pills at school in their lunch break; my girlfriends did them after school; a boy I used to go about with was heavily involved with dealing coke. I remember going into his room one day and there were scales out and he was bagging it up. I've seen people sniff drugs; I've seen it all. I've seen people take heroin. We lost one of our pals to smack before his eighteenth birthday.

I could drink loads when I was younger, and smoke loads of fags, but I've never, ever done gear. I haven't smoked weed – nothing. Drugs have always scared me; the thought of feeling totally out of control and not being able to claw myself back is just not for me.

I was quite lucky, because I was never teased about being straight, or peer pressured into taking drugs. I was quite a big character at school and never felt as if I had to conform. I had my own little gang going on.

Also my mum was very open. When I was really young, there was loads of publicity around Leah Betts, an 18-year-old who took an ecstasy pill and died. It was such a waste. Her folks released a picture of her to warn people of the dangers of taking ecstasy. I'll never forget it.

My mum put it on the fridge.

'Mum, take the picture down,' I kept saying.

'No, it's there so that if you're ever thinking about taking an E, you'll remember what happened to her.'

I thought it was a bit over the top at the time, but maybe it worked because I've never ever taken anything.

Twenty years later, in 2015, I thought of Leah Betts when I was in Toronto looking into ecstasy production. That's where I discovered that a shortage of safrole oil – an essential element in the making of MDMA – was having fatal consequences on recreational drug users in the city. Safrole oil, which is extracted from the root-bark of endangered trees that grow in South and East Asia, was becoming hard to find because of a clampdown on its importation, so the MDMA cooks were starting to replace it with other chemicals. The problem was, they didn't always know what they were doing, or they cut corners, or used dodgy ingredients. MDMA had become a real danger drug in Canada.

I met Cathy McCormack, whose daughter Cheryl had died from taking a powerful mix of chemicals similar to MDMA called PMMA, which was sold to her as MDMA. Cathy was totally heartbroken by the death of her daughter, and Cheryl's story reminded me that you can never know what you're taking. Cheryl had taken MDMA many times before the night she died and thought she was fine with it, but there's no way of ever being truly certain about what you're putting into your system – unless you test it first.

A few days later, I spent time in Vancouver with Meg, who tested her pills before taking them. Over a period of three years, Meg had discovered her MDMA had been cut with a wide range of substances: heroin, meth, aspirin, sugar and Ritalin. It really highlighted the dangers for me: you think you're taking a relatively safe party drug, but you're actually downing smack and meth before you go out clubbing. Pure ecstasy in its cleanest form isn't particularly harmful, experts say. It's when it is cut with crap or key components are replaced that it becomes messy. So many kids die because they've no clue what they're taking; these pills are a cocktail for disaster. Unless you're a chemicals expert, you'll have absolutely no idea how they will impact your body.

Contamination is a problem that goes beyond ecstasy: heroin, coke and meth are all cut with unknown drugs to make them more profitable. In Vancouver I visited Insite, a safe place for addicts below a rehab centre, where people could take drugs under supervision. Anyone who overdosed there received instant medical attention and the addicts I spoke to were very grateful for the support, because 23 people had died locally within one year, after taking heroin laced with the pain-killer fentanyl.

In the US, Obama's government favoured taking a holistic approach to tackling the drug problem, focusing on prevention and treatment almost as much as fighting the producers, smugglers and dealers. But the 40-year war on drugs outlived his presidency and the US government is still spending billions every year trying to stop drugs flowing into the country, although clearly most of the drugs are still getting across the border. Addicts fill the US courts, hospitals and prisons; homicides are constantly on the rise and there are more drugs around than ever.

It's kind of weird that the US goes on funding and fighting the war on drugs in the way that it does, because the only real winners are the organised crime cartels. I saw it first hand in Mexico, where I went in 2015 to find out why it had become the world's largest producer of methamphetamine, also known as meth, crank and ice.

I was terrified for most of the shoot, because a lot of Mexico felt totally lawless. Sinaloa, in the north west, was pretty scary. One of the main meth-producing states, it was home to the world's most powerful organised crime syndicate, the Sinaloa cartel, whose leader in 2015 was the infamous drug kingpin, Joaquín Guzmán Loera, better known as El Chapo (Shorty).

Meth production shifted to Mexico after the US clamped down on sales of the chemicals needed to make it. Now the US only produces 10 to 20 per cent of the meth consumed in North America, but demand is on the increase. The US clampdown was a gift to the Mexican cartels, who are making billions supplying meth to the US.

The Sinaloa cartel is the wealthiest criminal organisation in the world. Patty, a fearless local journalist who has been reporting on the cartel for many years, told me that 60 per cent of Sinaloa's money is generated by the drug trade. Drug money keeps the economy going, as the gang bosses buy off judges, politicians and businesses – the cartels feed the state and the state feeds them back in an unstoppable cycle of corruption. Everything runs off the drugs trade.

The police are completely overstretched. One officer in the state police in Tijuana on the US–Mexico border, the busiest meth-smuggling route into the US, was quite open about the fact that the cartels had the upper hand. His unit was trying to tackle their city's meth problem at street level as well as block the smuggling route, and their resources were a drop in the ocean compared with the massively rich Sinaloa cartel. It was a losing battle. There was nothing he could do except keep trying.

And there were so many murders happening, all the time. In 2015 alone, there were 17,000 homicides in Mexico, and organised-crime-style killings probably accounted for 40 to 50 per cent of them. Being a hitman is a career path – they're called *sicarios* – and I met a guy who was on a monthly salary of $2,000 plus bonuses for his services. He had killed over 20 people, never knowing the reason why, although he guessed it was often about money. He found killing easy, he said. He was very matter-of-fact about it, which gave me an idea of how normalised this kind of behaviour is in Mexican society. Less than 2 per cent of murders end in conviction in Mexico.

'I'd like to do something else, but there's no other work here,' he said.

Everything seemed upside down in Sinaloa, where support for the cartel was strongest in some of the poorest communities in the state. I went into the barrios to meet a group of ladies who saw El Chapo as a saintly Robin Hood character because of his acts of charity towards the poor, even though their towns and cities were being devastated by drug-related violence.

'Chapo's people help us; they do,' one of them told me.

'He likes helping out poor people a lot,' another chipped in. 'It's not just us who think so. A lot of people think the same. He gives food and money. He doesn't come in person, but he sends his people.'

They laughed when I asked what the government did for them. 'They do whatever they want. They don't help people and it's not fair.'

It was confusing. The people in these communities were living on less than $5 a day and had more faith in the narco-traffickers than in the authorities.

El Chapo was said to run a very organised business, keeping chaos to a minimum. That makes him sound almost decent and legit, but it's close to a fair comment if you compare the Sinaloa cartel to what was going on in the state of Michoacán in the west of Mexico. Michoacán was all over the show when I was there. It felt a lot more chaotic, violent and ruthless than Sinaloa. The cartels were so out of control that ordinary people were forming vigilante groups to fight them, creating more violence in their attempts to stop the extortion and brutality. There were police and army patrolling the streets of the towns and cities. The atmosphere was really threatening. It felt like a war zone.

Ironically, one of the dominant cartels, the Knights Templar, claimed it had formed as a self-defence movement to protect Michoacán from the other cartels in Mexico. In reality, the *Templarios* created just as much mayhem and violence as the cartel it overtook, and it was a really sinister organisation. Its leader, El Chayo (The Rosary), was a murderer, extortionist, kidnapper and drug dealer who ran his cartel like a religious cult. Not only did he think he was a saint – he commissioned shrines to himself across the state – but I heard some terrible stories about initiation ceremonies at his stronghold.

I spent time with a priest who told me about a lad of 18 who had been present at one of these ceremonies. This poor lad had been forced to watch as a three-year-old girl was killed – and then he had been made to eat her beating heart.

When you're from Luton in England and this is not your reality, it gets to a point in a conversation like this where you think, I'm mentally spent. This is too strange to accept as reality.

Who has sat down and thought, I know what we need to do to get people to show they're hard enough to get into our gang! We're going to tell them they have to eat a three-year-old's fresh heart that has just been cut out of her body. Who?

El Chayo was clearly insane and finally his atrocities drove the ordinary people of Michoacán to arm themselves and start their own self-defence movement. But more people with guns only meant that the state was descending into further chaos. It was becoming a failed state.

I was nervous throughout the whole trip to Mexico, but I was super nervous in Michoacán. We were in really hairy areas where journalists had been beheaded and their heads been left on bus stops, their bodies hanging from bridges. It was a really hostile environment. We had a safety advisor with us and he was totally on top of his game, but still you can't help thinking, What if this goes wrong?

I felt very alone and sad and painfully homesick on that trip. I had split up with my boyfriend back home, my mum thought I was in San Diego because I didn't want her worrying and I wasn't getting on with one of the girls in the crew. I never lost sight of how lucky I was compared to a lot of the people I was meeting, but we were filming from the moment we got up at 6am to when we went to bed at 11pm, often feeling tired and hungry, and it's hard hearing really difficult stories for 16 to 17 hours a day, especially when you're frightened.

It's actually exhausting being frightened all of the time. When you're not scared, you can do anything. But everything is heightened when you're genuinely thinking, I could be killed at any moment.

One day, we went back to our hotel after filming a sequence – and it was a proper hotel, where I could have a bath, which felt like a luxury. I thought about going out to get a bagel, but felt a bit sleepy and lay on the bed, lulled into a false sense of security by the feeling that I was back in civilisation, with electricity and hot running water.

Suddenly I heard gunshots out of the window. You've got to be joking! I thought.

I jumped up and looked out of the window. Two cars were zooming along the street outside the hotel. They screeched to a halt and I heard another shot, and another. It was terrifying, because I didn't know if they were going to run into the hotel and start shooting again, or head off down the street. Thankfully, they sped off.

Another day, I spent time with Jaime, who had been photographing crime scenes for a local paper for 20 years. It was a terrifying experience going out with him on a call to a crime. You had no idea what was waiting for you when you got there.

We pulled up outside some shops and found a man covered in blood. He'd been attacked getting out of a taxi and was clearly traumatised. A young shop assistant came out on to the street to warn me about how violent the area was. Someone had been killed on the corner a couple of days before. They'd shot him 17 times.

'What are you doing here?' she asked.

Good question! I thought. What am I doing here?

'You're crazy. You're *loco*! It's very dangerous.'

I heard shouting. Every nerve in my body was screaming. I could feel this tightly wound tension in the air and was petrified about what would happen next. Get me out of here! I thought.

We went back to Jaime's studio, where there were thousands and thousands of photos of crime scenes he had photographed. A lot of them were utterly horrific.

'The people doing these things are protecting their territory,' he said. 'They can chop your head off. It's how they express themselves.'

He talked about bodies in garbage bags in the street; bodies with their index fingers cut off and shoved in their mouths, to mark out the victims suspected of 'pointing the finger'.

'When these people want to protect their interests, they're unstoppable,' he said.

Looking at his photos, it was hard to get a perspective on what was happening in Michoacán. Sometimes you can understand where the narcos are coming from. I sort of get men killing other men over money, power and drugs – it's not personal; it's business. That's just the way it is. I'm not condoning it for a second, but men are going to kill men;

adults will always kill adults. But when they start bringing kids and innocent people into it, you think, No, you've lost me now. Surely they should be off limits.

I really felt it when I went to meet Jorge and Luisa, whose 19-year-old daughter and baby grandson had disappeared in August 2014, along with 11 other members of their family, including several children. The bodies weren't found until December, in a mass grave on the farm where they were working as lime farmers. The adults had been shot in the head and thrown down a well; the children's heads had been crushed with stones and their bodies dumped. It was a horrifying, disgusting crime, committed for no apparent reason.

It was one of the saddest situations I've ever been involved in. Jorge and Luisa and the rest of their family were all sat around in a courtyard when I got there. I didn't know how to approach the interview, because it was unlikely that justice would ever be served or they would find out what happened to their babies.

In that situation, you can't say, 'Well, the likelihood is that you'll find the people who did this and they will be put in prison.' Because it's not true.

You can't say, 'I hope you can move on with your life.' Because they've no opportunities.

Jorge, the dad, had no idea why his family had been targeted. 'From childhood they worked in the fields with a machete harvesting lime trees. They were never wicked,' he said despairingly.

It was impossible to know. Maybe the family had refused to give their land over to the cartel. Maybe they didn't refuse, but made a mistake. Possibly they were just in the wrong place at the wrong time, or perhaps they were involved and they weren't telling me the whole story. But even if that was the case, why kill the babies? Whatever happened, it resulted in the murders of numerous kids and no one being held accountable.

Luisa, the mum, was just in bits, the pain etched all over her face. 'We just ask, why did they do this?' she wept, clutching a photograph of her daughter. 'Why, if there were kids there? And all the family? I ask myself why? They took my daughter, grandson, son-in-law, my brother and all my nephews. Since then I've been unwell, always unwell.'

It's beyond comprehension. You can't understand how, as humans, we got here. If they rocked the boat and demanded answers, they might be risking retaliation. Their only option was to silently grieve. It just felt very, very hopeless. It was a very intense, very grim day.

The situation I saw in Mexico was totally shocking. The violence and corruption generated by the drugs trade was way out of control. One hundred thousand people had been murdered in a decade of drug wars. Corruption was at crazy levels. But the US drugs policy remained the same.

I've been all around the world looking into narco trafficking and drug use and I feel the war on drugs has failed spectacularly. I've spoken to experts in Canada, America, Europe and Asia and they all say the same thing: more people die because of the illegal market than they do consuming the drugs; more people are killed in the movement and dealing of drugs than the consumption of them.

I was totally anti-drugs when I started out exploring the subject. Now I'm wholeheartedly for change. Hearing the stories of people who have lost loved ones, either through taking drugs that proved to be lethal or at the hands of the violent cartels that run the illegal drugs trade, has made me think that there is a conversation to be had about potentially legalising certain drugs – or at least about making sure they're clean and people know what they're taking. Kids are dying – we're haemorrhaging kids – because there is this cloud of confusion. The dealers and gangs have all of the power and that power needs to shift.

Some people who argue this point have an agenda because they take gear on the weekends. But I haven't even experimented, so I have no personal desire to get my hands on any type of drug – I don't even drink or smoke. I just feel that if we did legalise certain drugs, people wouldn't be so vulnerable and a lot of the criminals wouldn't have a place in society anymore. I'm not talking about heroin, which devastates lives. I can't see there is ever a space for that in a healthy society. Clearly, not all drugs are the same.

I think the rules that are currently in place are such a failure. There needs to be an acceptance, however hesitant, that people will always take drugs and that people will always be willing to give them the drugs. So, if we legalise certain drugs or we at least think about this issue in a radical way, we might save more lives. We will still lose lives because drugs aren't safe, but we might lose far fewer than we are losing now.

4

Daisy

Child abuse

I have often felt pure hatred towards paedophiles. They're the lowest of the low, aren't they? You can't despise anyone more than somebody who abuses a baby or a kid. I've been sat in front of people I'm interviewing and thought, I would love to rip your head off. I would literally like to take your head off right now.

But none of that is going to make the kids any safer, or make things right, so I have to be quite self-disciplined. It's very easy to feel hatred – I understand that, because I've felt it. But the way I see it, hate is never going to solve anything.

It's a point of view that was tested to the limit in 2015 when I travelled to the Philippines to make a film about online child sexual abuse. It was my first time in the country and I was shocked by what I saw. The rise of cheap internet access had taken child abuse and exploitation to a whole new level in South East Asia. I'd seen it in Thailand, but international attention had forced Thailand to get to grips with it and things were getting better there. I'd seen it in Cambodia too, but when the heat was turned on Cambodia it moved to the Philippines, now the poorest of these three countries. Some of the abuse I heard about while I was there is unimaginable.

We had the idea for the documentary when we heard about Sweetie, a ten-year-old Filipina who'd attracted a lot of attention online in 2013. Sweetie looked so, so realistic, but she was actually a computer simulation operated by a group of specially trained researchers at a Dutch charity. They set up a paedophile sting operation using Sweetie as bait. Her profile was posted online in chatrooms around the world to see what the response would be. You couldn't tell she was an avatar at all. She really and truly looked like a real child.

The company that created Sweetie decided to make her Filipina after finding in tests that young South East Asian girls were more clicked on than any other type – more than young Eastern European girls, Western European girls, South American girls and African girls. They discovered this real appetite for young girls from South East Asia.

The moment Sweetie came online she was swamped by predators asking her to undress, play with herself and have sex with her siblings. In just over two months, 20,000 people contacted her and Sweetie's creators were eventually able to hand over a thousand paedophiles' names and addresses to police in 70 countries.

The UN and the FBI estimate that there are 750,000 people online at any given time who are interested in having sex with children. It's one of the most shocking things I've ever heard.

You always think it's a fat, old, grey man, but these online predators are men of all ages: they have jobs, kids, partners and homes. They do DIY at weekends; you meet them at the bus stop. It's scary. Paedophiles can be youngsters too – there are loads of guys in their twenties who go to Cambodia and the Philippines looking for sex with small boys as well as small girls.

Operation Sweetie led to eight potential convictions – in the UK, Poland and Belgium. It doesn't seem like many, after all that work and all those leads, but at least there are six fewer predators out there looking to abuse kids. Still, it's depressing that the conviction rates are so low. It's a whole new crime wave and the authorities can't seem to keep up.

I had to wonder, though. How do you tackle a problem so massive and widespread? Is it just up to the police and lawmakers – or is it a wider responsibility?

I met Daisy in a cyber café in Cebu City. It was a brick shed really, very unsophisticated, but the Wi-Fi was high speed. Loads of kids were sitting in front of computers paying one peso for five minutes on the web.

Daisy was 14 and often spent her evenings in chatrooms online. She was constantly being approached by foreign men. She was just about to tell me about the latest guy who had contacted her when a new man popped up on the screen. 'Let's meet in your city,' he wrote. He was 41.

Wi-Fi is really taking off in the Philippines, so it's getting easier for these guys to get in touch. And when the cybersex element isn't enough for them, they are flying over there for hands-on abuse. Daisy actually met up with one of them, an American, who paid her $30 for sex. The meeting was very traumatic for her, but she did it to help her family. It was hard to tell whether she would consider doing it again. She was so young – I think it would just depend on how desperate she and her family were.

She wasn't a lone case; she was one of thousands of kids in the Philippines who are online talking to white Western men after school each day. A lot of them are living in appalling conditions – in tents under a bridge or in home-made shacks. They've never got any food. Materialistic things aren't within their reach, so they speak to these guys hoping that they will ultimately get money from them. In their minds, money will bring them joy. It will stop the pain and the suffering. As they see it, these men hold the key to their happiness. They view them as walking ATM machines.

They are kids and they want the same as every child. They want fancy things and they want ice cream; they want to be taken out for burger and chips. So they end up justifying it to themselves. They think, *If I just do this, I can have a new pair of shoes.* When you've got a man who's being kind to you, as you see it, and he's saying he'll get you this and he'll get you that, 'and all you have to do is touch my dick or suck my dick,' you might think, *Well, is it so awful?*

Of course, they're not of an age to make that choice, because they're kids. They're vulnerable. They don't know they're being exploited. Sometimes their parents aren't aware of what they're up to, either.

Daisy told me that girls compete against each other to chat to Westerners online; it's a battle to attract these walking ATM machines. But they don't get paid just for talking; they only get given any money when they meet them or when they put shows on for the guys online. It's a meet up or a show; nothing else. And Cebu is a real hotbed for this kind of abuse.

I found myself thinking, *If I was in Daisy's situation, living here, in this slum, and I had nothing, what would I do?* You start putting weird boundaries in your mind as to how far you would go: *I would do this, but I wouldn't do that,* depending on the circumstances.

It's dangerous for the kids to meet these men, though. Some of them never get home. There are guys out there who don't just want sex with children – they want to hurt them, or worse. They target kids in the Philippines because life is so difficult there that the girls are willing to do horrendous things for next to nothing and the men can get away with a lot more because of the low conviction rates. It's a win–win situation for these guys. If you were a paedophile who wanted to harm children, you'd fancy your chances much more in South East Asia than you would in Europe or the US.

Daisy was being helped by a charity that would hopefully help protect her from the sex trade, but it's a stretch to help the thousands of other kids being groomed for cybersex and trafficked into online prostitution. To understand the scale of the problem, you only have to know that 500 children are intercepted every month at Cebu Port, where they often arrive with – or are met by – people claiming to be relatives or friends. Sometimes they've been tricked into leaving home and going to the city with a promise of a job or further education; other times their parents or other family members have sold them.

They say things like, 'I'm going to waitress for my uncle.'

'What's your uncle's name?

'Er, I can't remember …'

The kids who aren't rescued can face unimaginable horrors, headed straight to a brothel or forced to live in cybersex dens where they are abused in front of webcams on a daily basis. In some cases they are badly hurt or killed in the process – often to order, as dictated by paying clients in the West.

I'm not sure Daisy knew that she had a namesake at the centre of one of the most horrific cases of online child abuse in the history of the internet. The other Daisy was abducted by Peter Scully, an Australian who went to the Philippines and made a series of pay-per-view video streams of children being sexually abused. The worst of these was 'Daisy's Destruction', which was basically the utter annihilation of a child he called Daisy, which he filmed and distributed through the dark web. Loads of people tuned in to see him locking Daisy in a room and raping her and torturing her over and over again. Eventually she died.

It's just so unbelievable that anyone would want to watch that.

'Daisy's Destruction' was filmed in 2012, but Scully wasn't arrested until 2015. It makes me so angry to think he's still alive and kicking and the poor kid is dead. It's so unfair, so sad.

One of the biggest problems is that the Philippines is made up of more than 7,000 islands – so as soon as a cybersex operator has pissed off enough people and kicked up a bit of a storm in one place, they can just move their operation somewhere else even more remote. It's very difficult to trace these people. The situation is so serious that police forces all over the world are collaborating with the Philippine authorities to track down abusers across the country. I met several US Homeland Security Investigations (HSI) agents while I was out there. They were working undercover and supplying evidence to the Philippine Anti-Human Trafficking Division.

I went along with Philippine Agent Janet Francisco as she followed a SWAT team raid on a suspected cybersex den. For some time the suspect had been recruiting and abusing girls as young as eight online; now he was offering them up for sex to the undercover agents. Imagine selling an eight-year-old for sex with an adult man – it's unbelievably repellent. He was a horrific abuser and that morning had live-streamed himself having sex with a young girl.

As our car sped along behind the SWAT team van, I could feel my adrenaline pumping and my heart thumping. I didn't know what to expect.

I asked Agent Francisco if she was feeling nervous.

'No, I'm mad,' she said through clenched teeth.

When the SWAT team burst into the suspect's house, they found eight young girls, sobbing and crying out for help. One of them was so tiny it broke my heart.

While the girls were taken to safe houses by social workers and the police started to sift through the house for evidence, I was given permission to speak to the suspect. I was gobsmacked when he began talking to me. I was waiting for someone to tell me to stop asking him questions, or for him to refuse to give any more answers, but I kept my head and tried to get as much out of him as I possibly could. It was so bizarre – I couldn't believe how calm he was. He seemed so removed from the whole situation. There was no remorse. He was vacant and unresponsive. It was as if he didn't understand the enormity of what he'd put these kids through.

He said something like, 'It's OK for you Westerners to judge us and to hold these morals, but you don't really understand the situation on the ground.'

It was bullshit. I mean, you can dress it up as culture or circumstances as much as you want, but child abuse is child abuse, and he wasn't accepting responsibility for it. He said he had done it 'because of poverty', but he was studying to be a nurse, so clearly wasn't doing it to feed himself. And he was making a lot of money. There were receipts everywhere. He had loads of clients. It was pure greed. He was horrendous.

Sometimes the threat to these kids can be really close to home – just up the road, or next door, even. I went into a maximum security prison to meet Eileen Ontong, a woman who had been jailed for running a cybersex business using kids from her local neighbourhood.

Ontong was short, dumpy, middle-aged and looked like your aunt, but she was a monster. Originally a factory worker, married to a rickshaw driver, she recognised the earning potential of putting on cyberporn shows almost as soon as she learned how to use a computer. She began by exploiting members of her extended family, then things went so well that she began recruiting kids from her local area as well. Parents were coming to her saying, 'We need money. Use our kids.'

It's so hard to accept that these kids face danger everywhere, even at home, from their own mums. That's the worst scenario, I think, and when I hear about mothers offering up their kids for sex, online or offline, my first thought is, Sell yourself if that is your only option, if it is a choice between selling sex or your family starving! Put yourself up instead of your kids!

It is very easy for me to say this, sat in Brighton, in my comfortable house, but if I had children and I was in their situation, I would sell myself to feed the kids, however many times it took. If I had to have sex with 20 men, instead of my daughter having to talk to one man on a computer, I would do it.

I found it strange that some of the mothers I met weren't willing to do that. Maybe the market wasn't there, because they were older, but I find it hard to believe that you can't be a prostitute, as an adult, for other adults. It's what I would do in their situation, if there was no other way to feed my children.

It's easy to hate these women. You despise them for what they've done to these innocent babies. But then – and this is without condoning it in any way – I think it's a privilege, isn't it, to be in a position to be able to have morals? Because if you're literally starving, and you think your kids aren't going to eat unless you do this, then in some warped way you might justify it to yourself.

Some mums also justify it to themselves with the thought that the kids are so young they don't really know what's going on. They're thinking, I'm just stroking her vagina. It's not intrusive. At least it's me, her mother; it's not a foreign man or a stranger. She's only eight months old – or eight years old – and I can feed her as a result.

That's what they tell themselves – and it's what they say in their defence when they're caught. It's just so dark and so difficult. Sometimes, but not all of the time, I think it's circumstantial – that if the abusers weren't living in the Philippines and they weren't hit by poverty, things might be different. And some of them may well have been abused themselves as children and go on to continue the cycle of abuse.

The authorities are doing their best to tackle the problem, but they can't do anything about the social conditions that leave people so desperate that they'll sell their own babies into prostitution, or abuse them online for Western clients. It's very depressing. But sometimes, these crimes go beyond the circumstantial. When the authorities arrested Eileen Ontong, they found horrific images of more than 30 children aged between 5 and 15, and she was busted just as she was about to do a show with her daughter for her online clients. The police have since identified at least 20 people in the US, UK and Australia who paid her for online images or live shows.

I don't think you're ever born evil, but it's hard to know what had gone on in Ontong's life to make her so horrific. How much of it is learned behaviour, and how much of it is within you? No one seems to know. I went to visit her in prison because she had agreed to talk to me, but then at the last minute she changed her mind and refused to see me, so I wasn't able to ask her what motivated her. It was so frustrating that I wanted to scream – but perhaps she wouldn't have given me a straight answer, anyway.

Ontong's cellmate, Marisol Ayad, who had been jailed for similar crimes, swore to me that she'd been falsely accused by her neighbours. I later found out that she had operated a cybersex den using children between the ages of two and eleven. A two-year-old? It's unbearable to think of it. I just don't know how she could look me in the eye and claim she was innocent.

There seem to be two types of cybersex abusers: the people who justify it in their own minds as the only means to live; and people who are just evil, like Eileen Ontong and Marisol Ayad, who see it as a lucrative business and do it out of greed. The shit they put those kids through is unimaginable.

I saw it and felt it at a shelter for rescued girls about a hundred miles north of Manila. I sat in on an emotional expression therapy session, which gave abused and trafficked girls the space to release their pent-up feelings towards their abusers, who included their mums and other family members. It was really distressing to see young kids who had been happily playing an hour earlier now screaming, sobbing and punching the floor. 'I hate you, I hate you!' they yelled, their tiny frames hunched up in a corner, tears streaming down their cheeks.

Mary, the psychiatrist leading the session, said she knew from personal experience that this sort of therapy helped the girls to express their feelings about what had happened to them. It also helped them disclose the abuse to counsellors and social workers preparing statements for them. Mary had been sexually abused herself at the age of 12; anger therapy had helped her to move on.

But it was really difficult to watch these young girls reliving their pain and anger. We went back and forth as to whether or not we filmed it – but in the end I think you have to just show the truth and be as accurate as you possibly can. It's like, This is the reality.

These kids have been so devastated by what they've been through that they are very confused and unwell. They need psychiatric help. They need to release all of this anger that's been put on them by adults abusing them and built up inside them. So I'm pleased we filmed that sequence, because it was very telling. I just wanted the film to get across the horrendous, shattering consequences of child abuse.

I was blown away by people like Mary, who were completely committed to helping abused children – and also to the agents who dedicated their lives to bringing down their abusers. While we were in Cebu, we chanced on a couple of US Homeland Security agents at our hotel. It was a total coincidence. My director, Joyce, was sorting something out with our rooms and we got talking in reception.

It was just a friendly chat at first. 'How's things? What are you doing here?'

Obviously, their answers were very vague, because they couldn't give away details of their work.

'We're from the BBC, and we're making a documentary about child abuse,' I said.

We went on talking, but nothing too detailed. Later on, we were in contact with the Philippine authorities and they were working alongside HSI, so we met them again.

'Let's stay in touch,' I said, because I felt that there was so much more of this story to be told.

Everything was pointing to the fact that the horrendous issue of kids being abused, exploited and sold online was only going to get worse. So we kept in touch with HSI, back and forth, emailing and texting. Then, while Joyce and I were in Japan in 2016, they told us that they were planning to take down two sisters who were selling their children for sex – and would we like to cover it?

Of course we wanted to. But it was a hard sell to the channel. We had to convince the commissioner that the subject warranted a second trip to the Philippines. His response was a bit tepid. 'But we've seen all of this before, in the first episode. Why should we go back to it? What are you going to tell us that we don't already know?'

We really, really had to push for it.

'It's steadily getting worse,' I told him. 'These kids are being sold by their own mothers. We touched on it in the first documentary, but we didn't realise the scale of it and just how much it's happening. Now we've got unprecedented access with the Homeland Security. Please, just give us the chance to go back.'

Sensing I wasn't getting very far, I added, 'Look, if it's about money, or if you're not sure that it warrants an hour's film, we'll do a half-hour documentary and only go out for a week. We'll do it on the cheap.'

He went for it.

So we went back to the Philippines and I'm so, so glad we did. We met up with HSI and they were very generous with their time. Although they were in the middle of their operation, they allowed me to go everywhere with them. I wasn't briefed in any way. There were no questions I wasn't allowed to ask. They were just really honest and personable, and so desperately wanting to save people.

I found them completely awesome. They dedicate so much of their lives and sacrifice so much to save kids they don't even know. I really, really love these guys. They are such troopers, and really decent men.

One of them was called Mike. At least, that's what we called him. I don't think he'll mind me telling you this: he was very happily married, his wife was a sweetheart and he had two kids at home. He was a very upbeat guy when he wasn't talking about the case he was working on. We'd be joking about him and his family coming to England and us going to America, la, la, la.

But after a few days, I could see the draining effect of his work. He said that when he spoke to the Philippine children online, pretending to be a paedophile, he would think of his babies safe in bed, or at school, and the contrast would really upset him. Because it's just so unfair that one kid gets to live a beautiful, healthy, safe life and another kid is battered, tortured and raped, just because of the lottery of where they're born.

You can't help but compare, and you shouldn't, but you can't help but selfishly think, I got a good gig. It's just the luck of the draw where you're born and what your mother's going through at that particular time in her life. So you feel for these girls. It would be impossible not to.

I was with Mike as he negotiated with the mums, who were offering sex with their kids for less than $20. He was closing in, trying to arrange a meeting without spooking them. He was desperate to rescue the kids. I hated to think of how many kids had been sold for sex to Western men. Just the week before, a Brit named David Shepherd had been arrested in the south east of England for flying to the Philippines to have sex with kids. This ex-pub landlord from Dorset had raped children as young as eight and paid for and directed a huge number of live internet shows in which children under ten were sexually abused. His crimes were unbelievably horrific. There were so many different charges against him that the case had to be split into three trials. Thankfully, he was jailed for life – but how many other men like him are out there?

There was an atmosphere, a tension among everyone as the clock ticked down to catching these two sisters. It's hard to explain. You feel sick at what is to come. You feel devastated that you are about to do something that will tear a family apart and separate two mothers from their children, possibly for ever. But you also know it's totally the right thing for the kids, so it's a very confusing, conflicting situation. What makes it worse is that the children may not want to be rescued. They may not see it as being saved because kids generally want to be with their mothers, come what may. The whole thing is completely heartbreaking.

We were in the thick of this operation and they were raring to go when Mike got a text on his phone. It was his father-in-law saying that his little girl had hit the winning shot for her hockey team. Mike burst into tears. He was on the edge, so far away from home, missing his babies, and he just started sobbing.

'Are you alright?' I asked.

'My little girl just scored the winning goal,' he said, which, really and truly, isn't normally going to send a father into floods of tears. But emotions were running high. Everything felt so heightened, so enormous.

After the authorities pounced and their children were taken to safety, I interviewed the two sisters. They didn't ask how their kids were. They did not even ask, 'Where are my children? What's going to happen to them?' It was just all about them and how they had been tricked, and how Western men were to blame, and, 'Poor me. Poor me.'

That's where I found it very difficult, because I thought, Your kids are in a shelter now and you've not even accepted what you've done to them.

They wouldn't take responsibility. A few days later, when I went to meet one of them in prison, she kept saying, 'It wasn't me. It wasn't me,' – even though she had been caught in the act of selling her kids for sex to a Homeland Security agent, even though she had been arrested in a hotel room with her kids after arranging to meet Mike there. She was just completely lying about the fact that she'd put her kids through hell. It was very depressing.

People often ask how I cope in the face of such horrific realities. Fortunately my director, Joyce, is a good pal of mine, so after filming some of the conversations, we'd go and have something to eat and just talk about nonsense. You need to switch off or else you would drive yourself loopy, so we tend to focus on escapist topics like interiors and fashion. Blah, blah, blah. But a few times over the last ten years I have thought, Shit, do I need to speak to somebody?

This second film I made in the Philippines is a really tough watch. It's probably one of the darkest films we've made, because it looks into just how many paedophiles there are in the world, the styles that some of them prefer and the level of fear that some of them get off on. It's quite astonishing.

At first I was worried it was going to be too dark. But I didn't want the edit to sanitise the issue, because the reality is horrific and these are the kids that are going through it. I don't care if it puts some people off watching. I'd rather fewer people saw it but it was out there in its complete truth. Fortunately, the channel agreed, and it all paid off, as the film turned out to be one of the best received, most popular, most watched documentaries I've worked on. I'm so glad that we pushed so hard to return to the Philippines to make it.

My boss, the controller of BBC3, rang me after seeing the final edit. 'It's so harrowing, so painfully sad,' he said. 'I just wanted to make sure that you don't feel like you need to speak to anyone. Do you feel OK?'

'Yes, I do.'

The channel are good like that. They always check in with me and say, 'Counselling is available. A therapist is there for you whenever you need them. This is the number, this is the person; give them a call.'

It's weird, because when I was younger, I think I would have felt a bit funny about speaking to somebody – I would have felt that it was a bit over the top, a bit over-dramatic. Now I really would have no qualms. If I felt I couldn't shift something on my own, I would definitely go and speak to someone.

So far, I haven't felt that I've needed to. At the minute, I feel like I'm on top of things. I feel like I soak it all up when I'm there, give everything I've got on location, and when I come home I leave it behind. You can't bring it home with you because if you clung on to all of that negativity and pain, I don't think you would be able to live a normal life.

I imagine it wouldn't be useful if I did drugs or drank excessively, given some of the situations I've put myself in. I've seen cameramen who I think self-medicate to a certain extent. They drink and drink – and it might be that they're trying to block certain things out. There's no shame in that. I don't judge them in any way. But I think it's handy that I'm quite clear in my head.

I've worked with lots of directors who are very 'earth, wind and fire' and I adore them. They wear certain stones around their necks to keep the bad spirits away and stuff like that. I think: Whatever works for you! For me, a healthy way of processing it is by having these conversations with people, making sure they were worthwhile, coming away and digesting everything properly, shaking it off and leaving it there before going forward.

I'm always thinking about what can be done to stop child abuse, though. Some people argue that you won't stop it until the appetite for it goes away, but I can't see that happening. There will always be paedophiles. There will always be individuals who want to abuse kids and there will always be desperate people who are willing to do anything for money. As long as both parties exist, we will have these issues, unfortunately.

So I'm under no illusion that we can get rid of this problem and everyone involved with it. What I say is, Let's make it as difficult as humanly possible to abuse children and protect kids as much as we can. The UK, as a privileged country – one of the richest in the world – surely has a huge part to play. I think we have a moral responsibility to look after children all around the world. There are many people, especially now, who don't share this view, but I fiercely believe it.

A white Western child is no more precious than a poor Asian child. They're all kids. So we need to invest in protecting exploited and abused children overseas as well as at home, especially because so many of the perpetrators are British. More than a hundred paedophiles identified by the Operation Sweetie sting were from the UK – 110, to be exact. In 2014, the police investigated 139 Brits suspected of paying to watch Filipino children being abused online and that's probably just the tip of the iceberg. It's our men doing this. Our people are going over there, or paying to watch these shows. Why on earth aren't we more involved in stopping them? We have to hold them accountable to the law and make an example of them, and show that we are not going to accept paedophilia. Child abuse in the Philippines wouldn't be anywhere near such a problem without the demand for it from the West, so we need to say, as with the case of David Shepherd, 'We are taking this seriously. You'll get life.'

UK police chiefs are also starting to say that this is an issue that goes beyond law enforcement. There are so many people looking at images of child abuse online that we need to take responsibility for it as a society and have a proper debate about it. It's easy to look at a paedophile and wish them dead, but we can't just go around killing people, and our fury, however justified, won't solve the problem.

It's frightening how many paedophiles there are. Dave Thompson, the Chief Constable of the West Midlands Police, told the Commons Home Affairs Committee in 2017 that: 'The amount of men in this country who appear to show an active interest in this area is horrifying and the scale of it, I think, takes my breath away.'

Since the majority of online child-porn offenders don't get given prison sentences, what can we do to deter them? Many paedophiles are so ashamed and mortified by their desires that they can't admit that they are attracted to children, so perhaps one route is to fund charities that are in a position to talk these people through their feelings and help them to come out and openly say what's going on. That might sound quite radical and overly liberal to people who just despise these men, so you might have a tough time trying to go down that road. But the fact is that charities like Stop it Now, who work to prevent child sexual abuse, are doing some really important work in this area. Among other things, they provide a confidential helpline for people worried about their online behaviour and help them to stop internet offending.

I've spoken to people who say, 'No part of me wants to act on these feelings, but I can't help myself. I'm doing my own head in. Please make me better.'

When you hear that, you can't help but think, Well, they've been really honest and transparent. They don't want to feel like this. It's an illness. They need help.

Should you lock up people who are ill, or should you treat them? Can they even be treated? Clearly there is a distinction to be drawn between men who have abused children and those who have felt a sexual attraction but not acted on it, but how do you stop them potentially acting out their desires? There's so much more for me to learn about this.

We just need to be a bit more forward-thinking, I think. It's vital to raise awareness, and this issue has to be at the forefront of everyone's minds. We need trained specialists in this area – within the police and social services – who can help to hold people accountable when they are internet offending, because so often it's an anonymous crime, with few, if any, consequences. If you need to invest in those specialists, that's where you spend the money, in my opinion. There are already charities like Circles UK that provide a 'circle of support and accountability' around newly released sex offenders, with the help of volunteers, to help stop them reoffending. More needs to be done to prevent paedophiles acting on their feelings in the first place, online and IRL.

And let's hold the companies that make so much money from social networking sites and apps accountable, because they are all used by paedophiles. Let's ask, 'Where on earth is your duty of care? You're making all this money and you know kids run towards your apps. You know that there are adult men sitting there, waiting to abuse these kids on legit, legal apps. Not the dark web, but perfectly legal apps. And you're not willing to invest in more staff and more people to try to take these men down? WTF?'

These massive companies have a moral responsibility to try to shut down online child abuse. Anyone who can do anything at all to stop it has that same responsibility. The idea that they can say, 'It's the wild west. We can't manage everything,' is just not good enough. No.

We find it hard to accept that so many people have paedophilic tendencies. But they live among us and we've almost certainly come across some of them in our lifetimes. We have to accept that there are just so many of them. In 2015, the National Crime Agency estimated that there are 750,000 men living in Britain who have an interest in having sex with children, and a third of them are sexually attracted to children under 12. That isn't to say that these men necessarily act on their interest or attraction, but the NSPCC website cites a study that claims one in 20 children in the UK have been sexually abused, so the problem is widespread. In 2016, the NSPCC referred an average of 90 calls a week to police and social services over concerns that a young person had been sexually assaulted.

Like everyone else, I'm back and forth. When I speak to people who are attracted to kids, I sometimes feel a rash coming up on my neck, because everything they're saying makes me feel I want to vomit. Especially when I've just left a couple of kids who've told me that they've been abused for years and it's totally devastated them and ruined their lives.

You want to strangle these paedophiles. You do. You hate what they are. But then another part of you appreciates that in many cases they can't help feeling like this, and they're often tormenting themselves. They key thing is to stop them offending, but there's no black and white answer and it's not something you can simply fix or mend. It's so multi-layered.

Hating somebody or something isn't going to solve anything, though. So we're going to have to look at other ways of getting around it. Hate has never solved anything. It's a very unhelpful feeling. It's natural, but it's not useful. You can have it and hold it, but then you have to get beyond it.

Hate doesn't keep kids safe – and keeping kids safe is what matters.

5

Heydi

Femicide

I had never heard of femicide before I went to Honduras in 2015. I didn't even know it was a word.

At the time, San Pedro Sula in Honduras was the most dangerous place in the world to be female. Three women were killed or disappeared across the country every day. Domestic abuse was sky high and the leading cause of death among women under 24 was murder.

Imagine that.

Imagine saying to your mate, 'I'm just popping to the shops.' And her saying, 'OK, just make sure you don't get shot while you're out, won't you?'

Or you saying, 'I'm seeing my boyfriend later,' and her saying, 'Hope he doesn't kill you.'

I couldn't imagine it. Then I met Heydi Hernández.

I'll never forget Heydi. She was a real sweetheart: very warm and tactile, a beautiful Latin girl in her twenties who used to love putting on her high heels and going out. I sat and listened in disbelief as she told me her story.

'My husband said he was tired of being with me,' she recalled, fighting back tears. 'I told him, "If you are that fed up, then let me leave."'

After years of being in a violent relationship with this man who had always taken her for granted, she was desperate to get away. But he wasn't having it. Instead she saw him pull a machete from under the bed. He said, 'I'm not going to let you leave me.'

While her two young daughters watched, he went for her with the machete and hacked off one of her legs at the ankle and the other mid-calf, leaving her with two bloody stumps and a massive gash across one thigh. He made sure she couldn't leave. She literally couldn't walk away.

Now, I heard some horrifying stories while I was making a programme about domestic abuse in the UK, but nothing matched the brutality of Heydi's case. It's a miracle she survived, considering how much blood she lost and how determined her husband was to kill her. I met her a month after the attack, just after she'd come out of hospital, and she was still in shock, still trying to deal with what he'd done to her and the fact that she was never going to walk unaided again. She was sitting in a home-made wheelchair – a sort of plastic garden chair on wheels – and had to rely on her folks to help her around.

It was a real testament to her strength and courage that she was willing to speak to me. The expression in her dark brown eyes told me she was really suffering and yet she answered my questions with gentle consideration. I tried not to look at her legs while we were talking, because she was clearly embarrassed about the state of them. You could see they had been stitched up in a hurry – the scars were ragged and uneven – and she was horribly conscious of how lopsided they were. But the surgeon who saved her life was pleased with her progress. He said she was healing well, against all the odds.

Heydi was amazing, my *amiga.* I often think of her.

Attacks like this were happening all over Honduras when I made the trip there. Men were using machetes to chop up their wives; people were used to seeing it in the news. On my first day in San Pedro Sula, the newspapers were filled with reports of murders that had been committed in the previous 24 hours. And one front page was dominated by a recent mass protest against the violence.

'We have had enough! Stop killing our women,' the headline shouted. 'We keep finding our women dead in rubbish bags. They are not rubbish.'

It was mind blowing. I couldn't believe I was even reading these words.

Heydi's family encouraged her to talk to me because they wanted justice for their daughter. They were hoping her husband would face the maximum possible penalty behind bars. They were too poor to hire a lawyer, so they consulted a women's rights organisation for advice, because there was nowhere else to turn. I went with them to a meeting at the NGO to find out how the case was going.

Heydi's dad struggled to get her wheelchair up the stairs into the ramshackle building that serves as the NGO headquarters. The women who run this organisation are incredible; even though they are barely funded and face harsh criticism from all sides for the work they do, nothing will stop them fighting to improve life for their Honduran sisters. They were especially passionate about helping Heydi because they knew that without them she would have no one officially on her side.

But they looked downcast as they updated us about what was happening with the case. One of them held Heydi's hand across the table and squeezed it as she broke the news. 'The information we have from the district attorney's office is that they are only going to charge your partner with grievous bodily harm,' she said. 'I'm afraid it means he could be out of prison in less than two years.'

I couldn't believe it. At first I thought I'd heard her wrong. Two years?

Heydi's mum and dad were horrified. 'This isn't just bodily harm!' her dad protested. 'He cut up her life, not just her legs, and it's so sad to see her like this every day that I just can't take it.'

Heydi remained calm, though. Perhaps it was the shock, but it seemed almost as if she was resigned to not getting justice; she didn't seem surprised when the NGO women explained that fewer than 3 per cent of domestic violence cases are resolved in Honduras. I found this statistic astonishing. Could it really be true? In fact, it's absolutely correct: 95 to 97 per cent of cases of violence against women in Honduras won't end with a conviction. No punishment, no justice. There was a possibility Heydi's husband could be out within months, even weeks.

'If this man does get out earlier and he comes back or makes more threats, are you in a position to be able to help her?' I asked the NGO women.

Heydi's advocate looked at me helplessly. 'It's not easy to offer a solution in this country because justice almost doesn't exist,' she said.

What is going on here? I thought angrily. A woman has her legs cut off and the man who did it walks free? He should be sat in prison for years and years for what he did to her. No punishment, no justice and no deterrent. It seemed like if he wanted, he could come back and finish the job off, and no one would do a thing.

I was starting to understand why the levels of violence against women were so high in Honduras. Basically, the law was sending out a message to men that it wasn't a serious offence. It was giving brutal, bullying men the thumbs up to kick on and do what they want, because the chances of them spending time in prison were realistically very slim.

What was there to stop you killing a woman if she pissed you off?

Unfortunately, the Honduran legal system mirrors the Honduran culture. As in many of the countries of South and Central America, the idea that men are superior to women is deeply embedded. There are strict conventions governing the behaviour of the sexes: men are expected to be strong, proud and hyper-masculine, or 'macho'; women are supposed to behave like the Virgin Mary, or try to.

At best, the macho man sees himself as the strong, moral leader, provider and protector of his family. Meanwhile, his submissive, morally virtuous wife stays at home to cook, clean and look after children. It's an unrealistic behaviour model, especially in the twenty-first century, and men and women often struggle to live up to their designated roles. That's when machismo turns toxic.

The situation is made worse by the fact that everybody is up against it in Honduras right now. It's a major stopover on the trafficking route between South and North America; organised crime is massive, the cartels are rife and street gangs are fighting vicious turf wars across the cities. Two-thirds of the population – 4.5 million people – live in poverty, without reliable sources of food, energy and running water, and the hospitals are stretched to breaking point. It feels as if the whole country is on its knees.

In among all this madness, when it's difficult for guys to deliver what they believe a man should provide – money, comfort and protection – they reach for other ways to prove their manliness. It's the flipside of machismo – instead of protecting women, they harm and kill them, especially if they feel they can't control them. Clearly the women bear the brunt of it, but men are also victims of the macho mindset that is central to Honduras's problems.

Honduras felt scary and chaotic from the moment I arrived. People were talking about femicide everywhere I turned. Femicide – sometimes known as feminicide – is the intentional killing of females by males because they are females. It is a hate crime, but instead of being racist or homophobic, it is sexist.

There's nothing new about it, except for the definition, which emerged in the mid-1970s and gained wider usage this century. A rape that results in death is femicide, and the same goes for prostitution, sexual slavery and child sexual abuse that leads to fatality. In a wider global context, honour and dowry-related killings, female genital mutilation and the murder of unwanted baby girls are all considered to be femicides.

Femicide and domestic abuse go hand in hand. Cases like Heydi's don't begin with murder or attempted murder, they start with psychological, emotional or physical abuse that leads to violent injury or death. Because of the low punishment rates, domestic abuse rates are as high as one in two in some areas of Honduras and women have had to accept it as part of life. They are left with a stark choice, especially if they've grown up without the opportunity to get an education or earn money. Without state support – and there is none – it is virtually impossible for them to leave a violent relationship if they can't provide for themselves and their children.

If there is nothing to stop your husband mistreating you – if society tolerates it and the law won't protect you – you're most likely going to think: I'd rather be beaten up on a daily basis than lose my legs trying to get away. It is depressing that so many women are forced to accept this state of affairs, and are unable to turn to the law for protection and to the state for support.

Back in 2013, it looked as if the government might be getting serious about tackling the problem. The National Congress of Honduras approved a reform in the penal code which classified femicide as a felony carrying sentences of up to 40 years in prison. Millions were set aside in the following year's budget to set up a special femicide unit. But when I was in Honduras two years later, things were worse than ever. Heydi's case proved that justice was not being done. Nothing was being done. Why bother to pass a groundbreaking femicide law if you don't enforce it? I applied to the district attorney's office requesting an interview – and answers.

The culture of violence against women isn't confined to any one social group; it affects everyone, right across Honduran society. No one is exempt, it seems – not even the nation's sweetheart, the 'most beautiful woman in the country', 19-year-old María José Alvarado, who was crowned Miss Honduras in 2014.

María José was like a princess in Honduras. She was days away from leaving for London to compete in the Miss World contest when she and her sister, Sofía, aged 23, were shot dead at a party in November 2014. The lad who killed them was Sofía's boyfriend, Plutarco Ruiz, rumoured to be a major drug dealer with powerful connections. It was his party.

To this day, Sofía and María José's heartbroken mum, Teresa Muñoz, doesn't know why he did it. When I visited her at her home in Santa Bárbara, north-western Honduras, she softly sobbed as she showed me photos of her stunning daughters and talked me through María José's trophies and crowns. I felt devastated for her.

'I want him to tell me why he killed them,' she said eventually. 'He's never wanted to talk.'

I really felt for Teresa. She deserved answers, as anyone in her situation would. I asked if I could speak to Detective Reyes, who was in charge of the initial investigation into the shootings, and he agreed to take me to the club near Santa Bárbara where the sisters were murdered. At his insistence, we travelled there in a police patrol car with an armed escort, because it was too dangerous to go in a taxi. Honduras was starting to feel like a war zone, or the wild, wild west. It seemed totally lawless. People lived in fear.

On the journey, we talked about the rocketing numbers of violent deaths in Santa Bárbara. 'So many murders, mostly women,' Detective Reyes said mournfully. At the time, he was investigating the case of a man who had committed 15 femicides. One guy, 15 dead girls; you've got to question why they didn't catch him earlier.

We arrived at the place where the party had been held several months earlier, out in the countryside. The dance floor of the spa club where the Alvarado sisters were killed felt eerie and deserted in the daylight. Detective Reyes told me that there were about 30 people at the party when Plutarco saw Sofía dancing with another man and flew into a jealous rage. He got into an argument with her and shot her several times. When María José rushed to help her sister, he reloaded his gun and shot her at least 12 times.

'It's unbelievable,' I said, shivering.

He shrugged. 'In Honduras, it's common.'

It shouldn't be! I wanted to scream at him. Why can't you stop it? But in fairness, I think he was doing his best in difficult circumstances.

With inmates at the Bayview medium-security prison in Manhattan. There are more women locked up in the US than anywhere else in the world.

With inmates at Lakeview Shock Incarceration Facility in upstate New York, a voluntary programme where prisoners are drilled like soldiers and have every minute of the day timetabled.

Left: At the US–Mexico border in Sonora with Padre Prisciliano. The local gang members all respected the Padre, so he made sure we were protected during our stay.

Below: With Manuela, her son Jorge and their family friend Pedro in Sonora, Mexico. Manuela had paid a coyote $6,000 to take them from Guatemala to Los Angeles, but when she ran out of money he abandoned them at the border.

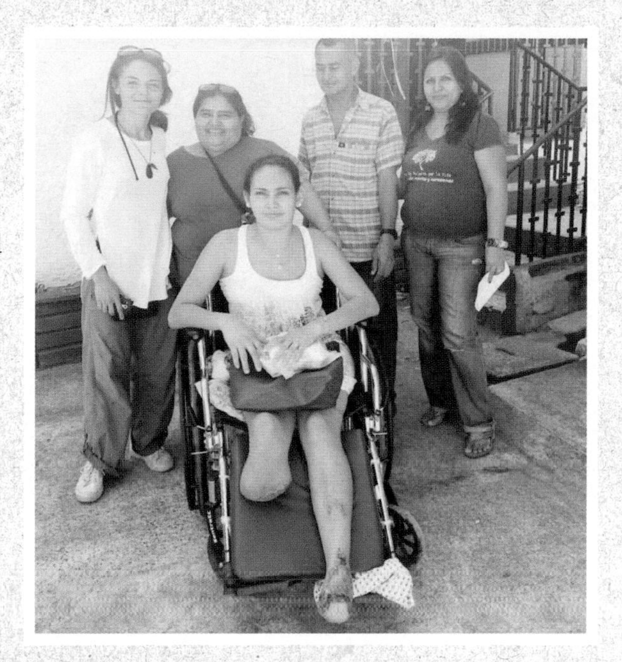

Right: With Heydi Hernández and her family in Honduras. Heydi's husband hacked off her legs with a machete when she threatened to leave him, but she'd learned that he could be out of prison within months.

Left: In Danlí prison, where 80 of the 600 inmates were serving time for violent crimes against women. Honduras's macho culture means many of these men thought they were completely justified in using violence to punish women.

Above: Yana was one of the 3 million Syrian refugees who had fled to Turkey since the war in Syria began. She had run a post office in Aleppo until the war, but now circumstances had forced her into prostitution.

Above: With trans sex worker Derya in Istanbul. Although it's legal to be trans in Turkey, trans sex workers are vulnerable to attacks, and these crimes often aren't taken seriously by police.

Right: With Babs and other trans sex workers in Rio de Janeiro. Because of the prejudice trans people face in Brazil, they're far more likely to do informal work like cleaning, hair and beauty, working in nightclubs or prostitution.

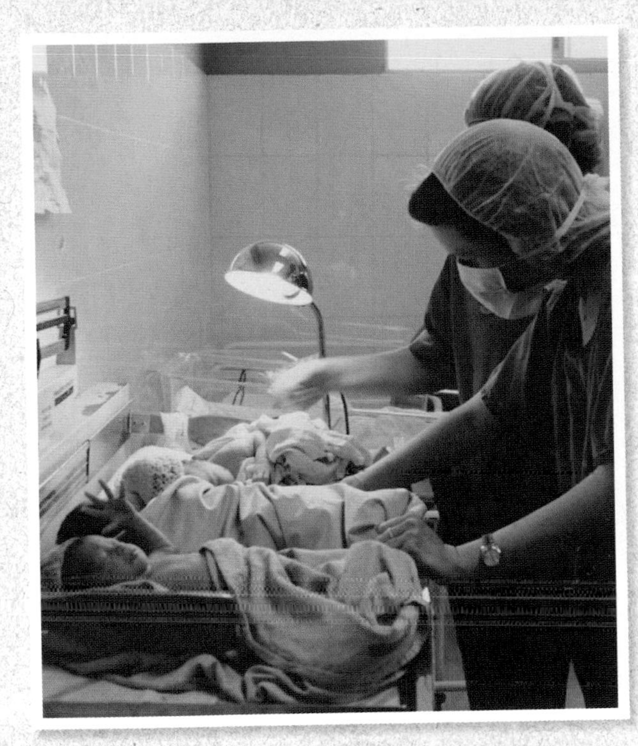

Left: The maternity ward in Honduras where 13-year-old Sylvia gave birth to her daughter. Every year 50,000 teenage mums give birth in Honduras, where abortion and contraccption have been illegal since 2009.

Above: Listening to an anti-abortion talk at a summer camp run by pro-life group Survivors in southern California. I was shocked by how young some of the participants were, and how easy they would be to manipulate.

With anime expert Dan Kanemitsu, who argued that banning X-rated manga images featuring child-like figures would infringe on free speech. I understood his argument, but couldn't get him to tell me why anyone would want to look at these images.

At a grave near the Highway of Tears in British Columbia, Canada, where nearly 40 women and girls have died or disappeared, many of them indigenous.

Above: With the Yazidi women in the Pershmerga Army, training for battle on the frontline. Many of them had escaped from captivity with Isis and wanted to rescue other women still being held hostage.

Above: Most of the Yazidi fighters had no military experience and had never thought of going into the army. They were just typical, relatable women.

Above: There were unexploded bombs everywhere we drove in Iraq, with slogans written on them saying things like, 'Isis will forever be in control.'

Above: Coming face to face with a convicted Isis killer in Sulaymaniyah prison in Iraqi Kurdistan.

Left: Questions Shereen wrote down in my notebook to ask the Isis member. Everyone was certain she was going to break down during the meeting, but she was so calm and dignified.

Above: With Shereen in the ruins of Mosul, where she was held hostage by an Isis fighter and his family.

There were 30 people at the party but no one dared to speak to the police – they were way too scared of Plutarco and his connections. Some of the men at the party even helped him to bury the bodies, which weren't discovered for six days.

María José's fame and the fact that she was shot so soon before the Miss World contest put international pressure on the Honduran authorities to investigate the murders. Eventually, Plutarco confessed and three years later was convicted of the femicide of Sofia and the homicide of María José. When he made his court appearances, he grinned at the crowds and the cameras. He's a celebrity now; he's got a lot of fans. It's totally weird.

It's hard to imagine what goes on in the heads of guys like Plutarco Ruiz and Heydi's husband. How do they manage to justify their crimes to themselves? I wanted to find out more, so I headed to Danlí prison in the south of the country, where I was told that 80 of the 600 prisoners were men serving time for violence against women. They were the ones I wanted to talk to.

Being one of the only women on the other side of the prison gates felt quite scary. It was one of the world's most dangerous prisons and I wasn't there to be nice to the inmates I was meeting – I intended to ask them why the hell they didn't respect the fundamental human rights of women and hold them equal to men. Well, in so many words! I just had to hope that the guards would have my back if any trouble broke out.

I was escorted to a cell packed with men – it was like a big cage at the zoo. The prisoners were living in cramped, dirty conditions and I thought, Wouldn't you do anything to avoid being locked up here?

Several guys tried to talk to me through the cell bars. The testosterone levels were through the roof. One charmer complimented me on my beautiful name and asked if I had a boyfriend.

'Tell me why you're inside,' I said.

'Rape,' he replied, quickly assuring me that he didn't do it.

'She is just lying?' I suggested.

A burly, tattooed bloke tried to give me an artificial red rose through the bars of another cell – because everyone has their romantic side, I guess.

'Oh, is that for me? *Muchas gracias*,' I said, without taking it.

None of the men I spoke to would admit to harming or killing a woman. So I had to ask them, you know, *theoretically*, why they thought some men were so violent towards women in Honduras?

'Because men don't like it when their chicks cheat on them,' one prisoner said, laughing. The other guys in the cell laughed along with him. I got the feeling it wasn't really a joke though.

The tattooed guy gave me a quick lesson in Honduran machismo. 'I can have three or four women but I have one main girl, the one I respect most, and I expect her to respect me back,' he explained. 'Let me tell you something,' he added in total seriousness, his voice dropping a tone. 'When a woman turns up dead, it's because she's done something.'

The guys around him nodded in agreement. Yes, it would definitely be her fault.

'If you love someone, you don't punish them; you don't hurt them; you don't murder them,' I stuttered.

He shook his head. 'When we love, we love with our whole heart and this is what makes us aggressive,' he said. 'We are scared that someone will come and break it.'

There was a pause and then he grinned. They all grinned. And no wonder. This was their let-out clause. They could justify violence and murder in the name of love. I got the feeling it was an idea they had grown up with.

'Wow. Remind me never to date a jealous Honduran man,' I said.

They laughed again.

Fortunately for me, I have a choice, I thought – but if you're a Honduran woman you have to live with this bullshit mentality.

I went inside the prison to interview Homer, who was serving 30 years for murder. He looked unremarkable, like a school caretaker, but in 2013 he slashed his wife's throat with a machete during an argument. She bled to death.

'She was cheating on me,' he said. 'Understand?'

I think, as far as he was concerned, it was all the explanation he needed to give. It was pretty simple in his eyes: she stepped out of line, he punished her.

But just in case I needed further proof of her guilt, he added, 'I told her to quit her job but she never wanted to obey me.'

Instead of being grateful to him for offering to be the sole provider, his wife wanted to go out and earn her own money. She didn't want to be stuck at home, cooking and cleaning. For this, he killed her. He saw it as his right. It was a crime of passion, he claimed, which in Honduras carries a lesser sentence than premeditated murder because in the eyes of the law that 'moment of madness' offers some justification for the outburst of violence. In my mind, it's completely crazy that killing someone who isn't trying to kill you can in any way be viewed as acceptable, but Homer talked about how his love and jealousy drove him to kill his wife as if it was natural and logical.

'But do jealousy and "passion" justify murder?' I asked.

'Yes,' he said, without hesitation. He looked at me like I was a moron for asking these questions. It was so straightforward to him.

He didn't show any guilt or remorse. He refused to take any responsibility for killing his wife. 'If she had behaved better, she wouldn't have provoked me to do this,' he said grimly.

It made me feel angry and frustrated to listen to him, but at least I had an idea of how he was thinking. He genuinely felt that his wife brought it on herself: it was her fault and she deserved to be murdered because she didn't behave in the way he expected her to. To him it was a totally rational response, so why didn't I get it? It was machismo at its very worst.

Men like Homer and Heydi's husband feel they have the absolute right to control the women they're with – the women they say they love – and this is how they defend themselves in court.

'I loved her so much that I couldn't bear to think of her with another man, so I cut her head off.'

It's completely mental; it doesn't make sense.

Like Homer, Heydi's husband claimed that Heydi pushed him into it. He said he cut off her legs in a moment of blind rage, which she triggered when she threatened to leave him.

'I am the man, I am powerful! You will listen to me!'

But he was lying. It wasn't a heat of the moment attack. It wasn't as if he stabbed or shot her and immediately regretted his decision. Cutting through flesh and bone takes real physical effort and time. He knew what he was doing. You really have to commit to sawing through someone's legs.

I couldn't help worrying about what would happen to Heydi if her husband was let out of prison. Would he come back to find her and kill her? Or pay someone to do it for him? Contract killing is one of the most common forms of femicide in Honduras. A husband or ex-boyfriend can hire a hitman for just a few dollars. Mostly, it happens when the women are at home. It's all over in seconds: a masked gunman will burst in, take aim, shoot and run away.

So where could Heydi and her kids flee if her husband came after her? It didn't take me long to discover that there are only three women's refuges in the whole of Honduras. I visited the oldest and biggest refuge, which had housed more than 4,000 women and their children in the 19 years it had been running. It was like a fortress – covered in barbed wire, with alarms and armed security. Ana Cruz, the boss, offered to show me around. But the whole place was deserted. It was like a ghost refuge. 'What's going on?' I asked Ana Cruz.

She explained that the previous year, the authorities had forced her to take in a woman wanted by the gangs. Knowing the risks, she objected, but they overruled her. A few days later, armed men stormed the building, wrapped the wanted woman in a quilt and kidnapped her and her infant child. They were never heard of again. And the craziest thing about it was that Ana Cruz was totally in the dark about whether the woman was kidnapped by gang members or by men sent by the district attorney. It was like something out of a movie – it didn't sound real.

'Welcome to Honduras!' she said with a bitter smile. 'This is how we live.'

Petrified by what happened, the other women in the refuge fled and it had remained shut ever since. So there were only two small refuges housing abused women in Honduras while I was there – in a country where three women were turning up dead every single day.

It started doing my head in: just the thought that every morning women up and down the country were waking up wondering if they would survive the day without being raped, beaten, tortured, shot or kidnapped. How did they manage to keep going?

Later, I visited the San Pedro Sula hospital morgue, where a forensic expert showed us around and talked about some of the problems Honduran women face, from domestic violence to preying gangs. Her manner was brisk and matter of fact – she saw these horrors day in day out – but I felt really sad to hear some of the stories. One doctor told me that girls as young as nine were being taken into hospital with gunshot wounds.

At the top of the building, there was a viewing gallery where surgeons and medical students could watch autopsies. Although looking at dead bodies makes me feel dizzy, I took a peek over the side because I felt I should and glimpsed a body on a table under glass. The flesh was on one side of the table; on the other were the organs that had been removed during the autopsy. They had been picking bullets out of the body. It was one of the most horrendous sights I've ever seen. 'I'm going to be sick,' I told Steph, the director. 'I've got to get out of here. Just give me two minutes.'

I ran outside and sat on the hospital steps to get some air and sort myself out. Just then, an ambulance arrived and a couple of paramedics started taking bodies out of the back – loads of them – including the bodies of young women. They threw them down for collection, but not in a disrespectful way – it was just that they need to get the job done because there were more to come.

I began to feel like there were dead bodies everywhere I looked. 'I can't take it anymore,' I told Steph, in tears. 'I keep imagining how awful their lives have been.'

Back in my hotel room, I sat on the bed listening to music, trying to digest the day's events. I needed to clear everything out of my mind before I went to sleep, so that I didn't take it with me in the morning. First, I had to accept that these things were happening. Also, that I can't save the world.

My job is to raise awareness, I thought. I mustn't hang on to what I've seen today, or I will drive myself insane.

It was rough. I listened to Little Mix, something frivolous, and texted my boyfriend Sam to say I loved him.

'How was your day?' I asked.

'Shit,' he replied. 'I got a parking ticket. I'm so gutted! How was yours?'

The next day, I got up early, ready to face the new day. Honduras is relentless, though. I wanted to know why the government wasn't doing more to protect women, but my attempts to meet with an official representative at the general attorney's office hit a wall. It was so frustrating. I wanted to cry. These were the people responsible for making sure that justice was served, but when I got there, the man they put forward decided not to speak to me. I explained that we were giving the authorities the right to reply to some of the allegations raised in our investigation of femicide and violence against women in Honduras. But he still refused to sit down and answer my questions, even though I arrived at the agreed time on the agreed day.

It was a damning reflection of the government's attitude to these problems. I was from the BBC and they completely blew me out, so imagine if you are a poor young girl from the barrios wanting to lodge a complaint. You've got no chance, have you?

Many Honduran girls feel that the only way to resist is to flee. Women crossing borders to escape violence and poverty is a trend throughout Central America – it's being called the feminisation of immigration – and in 2014, a total of 11,000 underage Honduran girls were stopped trying to cross the US border. You can't blame them, can you? I would do the same if I lived there, if I was poor and I was scared.

Apart from the thousands of dollars that they have to pay the coyotes and the dangerous trip across the border, the risk of being raped on the journey is so high that some of the women get illegal contraceptive implants before they leave, so that they won't get pregnant en route. They risk being kidnapped and killed; they are taking a potentially treacherous step into the unknown. And yet still they go.

In the middle of the night at the bus station in San Pedro Sula, I spotted a woman getting on a bus heading for Guatemala with four children in tow – but no luggage. She avoided my eye and moved away when I tried to speak to her. Somewhere in the shadows, a coyote was doubtless watching her. Her life was in his hands. She had no voice. She was completely vulnerable. I crossed my fingers for her, hoping she would make it.

But for some – for women like Heydi – it's too late to leave. All Heydi can do is sit and wait, hoping that a shift in her country's culture and attitudes will bring a better future for her daughters. I really hope that shift comes soon – and I hope that appearing on our film helped her in some way.

I was proud of the film we made in Honduras. By then I wasn't so bothered about what the critics said, but I'd be lying if I said I wasn't grateful when the late *Sunday Times* critic, A.A. Gill, wrote a beautiful piece about me and the Honduras documentary. It was the loveliest review saying I was a thorough journalist and a focused presenter. He said that I knew what I was talking about and ought to be on *Panorama*!

It was really unexpected. And because A.A. Gill was so well respected and everyone rated what he was saying, it changed things. There was an instant ripple effect. People noticed and started thinking, Oh well, if he's saying it, maybe she *has* got something.

Suddenly loads of other people were messaging me: 'Hi, I read what A.A. Gill said, blah, blah, blah.'

You're such sheep! I thought. But I really appreciated the write up. It was really kind – and it meant more people would watch the film and find out what was going on in Honduras.

6

From Avlora to Yana

High-end to low-end prostitution

When I think about prostitution, the polarising question that ALWAYS arises in my mind is, 'Is it empowering or is it degrading to sell your body?'

A decade ago, if you'd have asked me this same question, my answer would have been, 'Degrading, obviously.'

But now I think it depends on the circumstances. Every scenario or case is different. And I've come to this conclusion because of all of the conversations I've had and all of the relationships I've formed with sex workers around the world. I think that until you sit down with these girls and hear their stories, you can't really understand what they are about.

Take Avlora, a call girl I met in Moscow in 2016, while working on a series of films about sex and prostitution in Russia, Turkey and Brazil. Avlora was quite surprising. It can be hard to understand why a woman would truly choose to have sex for a living, but this is actually what she would prefer to do.

'I love my job,' she told me, and I believe she was being completely genuine.

She was dainty, blonde and super sweet – and in many ways she typified the global image of the high-class Russian prostitute. She travelled everywhere by chauffeured limo. She met her clients in Moscow's top luxury hotels. And in one night she could earn almost twice the average Russian monthly wage.

When I went to meet her at her apartment in a fancy high-rise block, she sat me down on her bed and proudly talked me through an album of glossy sex photos, explaining that she really, really loved having sex and took enormous pride in performing various acrobatics with multiple partners. 'I always wished to be beautiful in the eyes of others,' she told me. 'I used to be very shy, but after five years doing this job I'm sexier and more confident.'

'Oh, wow,' I said, as the threesomes popped up in front of my eyes. She said she was getting a name for herself in the Moscow porn industry – I could see why.

What fascinated me was that Avlora didn't seem to have any demons or psychological issues, which is what people often assume might be underlying a situation like hers. She was from a fairly well-off, comfy family and lived a nice, middle-class existence outside of her work.

She had trained to be a PA when she left school, but the job bored her. Prostitution appealed because she loved the sex, the money and everything that came with it. She loved the bags, the perfume and that she'd just bought a large apartment in the centre of the city. There was no part of me that felt she needed rescuing, or that she was trying to fool herself that this was OK. It was simply what she chose to do.

Many people find it hard to understand how someone would be able to totally separate sex and emotion, myself included. They look for a 'reason' or try to find an example of how this person is lost or hurt or exploited. Tellingly, the head of a high-class escort agency estimated to me that 80 per cent of his girls came from broken families or had suffered physical or mental abuse. But Avlora wasn't a chaotic, lost soul. She'd had a good education and was a functioning, contributing member of society. She didn't rely on anyone to keep her and honestly appeared very content with her lot.

I had a strong sense that she was in control and making her own choices. When I dropped in on a shoot for her website, she was the one calling the shots, not the top professional photographer she had hired to take her publicity photos. Wearing studs, stockings, suspenders and a mask, she dictated where and how explicitly she posed (to the max!) and appeared to love every minute of it.

'Like this!' she told him, posing inside a cage with her legs wide apart.

'Oh wow,' I said, again.

Everything was on her terms. Except, of course, when it came to providing a service to her clients. But she seemed to relish that side of things too. She told me she loved all kinds of sex, especially anal sex.

While we were having lunch one day, just before we dropped her to the airport, she went to the toilet halfway through her food and was gone ages. What's she doing in there? I wondered. Is she OK?

When she came back out she said, 'Oh, I was just cleaning my arsehole because I know I'm going to have anal sex when I meet my client in St Petersburg.' And then she got on with eating the rest of her lunch …

I've met quite a few women like Avlora – women who seemingly adore every aspect of having, or being associated, with sex. Among them is an ex-neighbour of mine, a woman in her late forties who was one of the UK's most recognisable porn stars. She was very 'normal' and sweet and we were mates – she used to let me scrounge her Wi-Fi and always put welcome-home cards through the door when I got back from my trips. She also happened to have intercourse with numerous people for a living.

Every Sunday I'd see all these pairs of Reebok Classics lined up outside her flat, because she made the men take their shoes off before they went inside. Then I'd hear them pounding away in her flat all day long, bang bang – there were fireworks going off in there and I'd be going to the shops to get some milk. She was hilarious; she could not get enough.

We expect this kind of desire to be more of a male thing, but these are women for whom sex consumes their everyday thinking – their world seems to revolve around either having sex themselves, or watching other individuals get down and dirty. I am awed by some of these women's sexual appetites. When I hear their stories, I think, My God, you're having sex six times a day! Who's got the time and energy? I've got to go to work, feed the dog, keep the house nice, pack …

The idea of being in an almost constant state of arousal is soooo foreign to me – and how are their minnies so perfectly waxed all of the time?!? – but there are a lot of women who live their lives this way. Bright, articulate, bilingual hookers have told me they'd much rather lie back and have sex than put on a suit and work the typical nine-to-five. An office job just doesn't appeal to them and will never be how they try and make their cash. I don't see a problem with that – why would I? Although their choices are light years away from mine, if what they do is safe and they're consenting, who am I to tell them how to go about their business?

'All jobs are difficult,' one of them told me. 'Better to be talking with a nice man than stuck with a nasty old lady behind a shop counter.'

I can see her point – if only it was a matter of just *talking* to the nice man.

I'm not for one minute suggesting that these women represent the majority of adult entertainers or sex workers. I'm under no illusion that there are far more people who have been pushed into that world than have chosen to jump, even at the high end of the sex trade.

In Brazil, where I spent time at the Bahamas Night Club, a luxury hotel where sex workers can rent out rooms to see their clients, one of the girls I spoke to seemed really sad that she had ended up there. Lara was absolutely stunning, one of the prettiest, sexiest women I've ever met. When she told me she owned a stationery shop, I found it hard to picture her selling notebooks and rulers. And yet she would have much preferred to be working in her shop than at the Bahamas Night Club, the Rolls-Royce of Brazilian brothels. She had a boyfriend who didn't know that she was prostituting herself on the side and she longed to spend her nights with him instead of the 'old guys and ugly guys' she was forcing herself to sleep with.

Financially, she was in a bit of a mess – not so bad that she couldn't buy rice or anything that extreme, but by her standards she was struggling. Her plan was to pay off her debts and get back on the straight and narrow as soon as she could. Like so many of the girls I've spoken to, prostitution was a means to an end, after which she intended to pack it all in.

'I need to make the best of a bad situation, put things right and move on,' she said. 'This will only be a brief chapter in my life.'

It's a line I've heard from so many girls in similar situations over the years. 'This isn't forever – I'll do it for a couple of years maximum. It's just until I sort myself out and get back on my feet. Then I'll turn my back on the whole industry.'

I think that's how I would probably feel if I found myself in their position. You hope there's more to life, don't you? Because you know you've got more to give. You think, Times are tough. It's just a difficult phase. Let me ride this wave out and then I'll start again.

But it's not always easy to get out. Sex workers operate on the fringes of society, where a normal life can seem harder to access, especially when you're working illegally and mixing with people on the wrong side of the law. Substance abuse is common – some sex workers self-medicate because they are unhappy, or because they never thought they'd find themselves in a situation where they had to sleep with people for money, so they sniff a bit of coke or drink themselves to oblivion to blank out having sex with guys they do not find remotely attractive. It's totally understandable. Imagine looking up and seeing this man on top of you – you'd want to be anywhere other than there, wouldn't you? But, as I was often told, 'Money doesn't grow on trees,' and, 'You've got to make the most of what you've got.'

I used to think that you could get too old for it, but I've met loads of older prostitutes. Often they are homeless, sadly. In Canada I met an 80-something hooker, a frail old woman who lived in a refuse bin and wore a curtain trim as her top. A lot of young guys went to see her. She was popular because she had no teeth and so could give really amazing blow jobs, they said. I met someone similar in Prague – the police introduced me to her. She had been around for decades and had a really good heart, they told me. She never robbed the guys who went to her, as other street prostitutes did, so they turned a blind eye because there was no other way for her to earn money.

And that's the bottom line, for most sex workers, whatever their age – they're doing it to survive. Very few prostitutes choose – really genuinely choose – to be there. More often than not, it's circumstantial. The high-class Russian call girl is a global fantasy, but most of the three million sex workers in Russia sell sex to pay the rent, feed their kids or just get by.

One of the charity workers handing out condoms and lubricants to prostitutes on the streets of St Petersburg summed it up simply by saying, 'When there is less money around, there are more women on the streets.'

These girls do it because they have to.

Prostitution is illegal in Russia. The number of sex workers grew after the breakdown of the Soviet Union, but the government is now trying to eliminate it, at least at street and brothel level. There appear to be some horrendous double standards at work, though. In a 2017 press conference, Putin half-joked that Russia had the best prostitutes in the world – and he probably had in mind glamorous girls like Avlora, who get round the law by calling themselves escorts and ostensibly charging clients for their time instead of for sex. No one bothers them, least of all the police. If anything, there could be a tacit admiration of their 'entrepreneurial drive'. But there are no such loopholes for the women who sell themselves on the streets. Not only are they criminalised by the law and shunned by society, there's no protection for them, either – and it's all part of a nationwide campaign against prostitution.

Sex workers on the streets put themselves in unbelievable danger when they go out to work, getting in and out of strangers' cars all night. I don't know how they deal with the fear, let alone the sex. While I was out one night talking to a couple of girls by the side of the road in St Petersburg, a sinister car drew up at the kerb, full of snarling men in black. The girls tensed up and I asked them if they'd like to wait in our van until the coast was clear. They gratefully accepted; you could sense their relief.

It was a total reality check for me to realise that if anything happened to these girls, they would have nowhere to turn.

They couldn't go to the police, because if they said they'd been attacked or raped while working the streets, they'd more likely be arrested than helped.

What made things worse was that the police seemed to be taking advantage of the situation. I actually saw some girls bribing a police patrol while I was out there. They gave them 500 roubles (£5) not to arrest them – it was the standard bribe at the time. And they weren't getting protection for that money, just permission to go on working illegally. The blatant corruption of it shocked me.

A £5 pay-off doesn't sound like a big deal until you realise that these women get £8 for giving a blow job and £12 for sex.

£8 for a blow job?

'How much would you charge?' one of the girls asked me, with a giggle. She seemed so much more relaxed once she was off the street and in our warm van.

'A lot more than that, let me tell you,' I said.

But if my kids were starving, or I had nowhere to live, the truth is that I might easily to do it for less. I met girls in Brazil who were sleeping with 30 guys a night, just to earn enough to live.

I couldn't confront the Russian police about the pay-offs they were demanding because it might endanger the girls, but I did manage to get an interview with an MP, Vitaly Milonov, a prominent, ultra conservative politician in St Petersburg. I called him out on the so-called war against prostitution in Russia, but in my opinion he seemed totally out of touch with the real world. He told me that his aim was effectively to stamp it out. If prostitutes needed financial support, he said, they would get it from the government as long as they promised never to sell sex again. It felt so patronising, so unrealistic.

Then, in the next breath, he said that prostitutes were no different from murderers, because they were breaking the law.

'They put themselves on the dark side,' he said dismissively. 'It's a sin. You cannot legalise it.'

It was mind blowing to hear him put sex workers in the same category as murderers. If a powerful state official was expressing such views, what hope was there for the girls on the street? I tried to appeal to his compassionate side by reminding him that these were vulnerable human beings we were discussing – his fellow citizens, risking their lives to earn their keep – but it was obvious to me that nothing would change his views. What made it worse was that there was a photo above his desk showing him cuddling a kitten. Pass the sick bag, I thought. He pretends to be kind and caring, but it looks to me like he has no compassion at all.

The street is by far the most dangerous place for any prostitute to work – and during the Russian winters, it is also bitingly cold. You're going to be a lot better off doing the job in the relative warmth and safety of a flat or house – or that's what I thought until I visited an illegal brothel that operates out of a flat in a rundown tower block on the outskirts of St Petersburg.

It was a grim building and I felt nervous as I made my way up the dank stairway towards the flat. Then, just as I was arriving at the door, I heard a skirmish.

One of the girls put her head out of the door and whispered, 'Stay quiet. Just wait a moment. We have a problem man inside. I will call for you.'

For the next ten minutes I waited breathlessly while the security guard evicted a client who had turned violent. It clearly wasn't a great time to go in and talk to the girls about their day-to-day lives, but it had taken weeks of negotiation to get this far and I didn't want to give up. So I stayed.

As it turned out, the girls were used to out-of-control clients. When I finally got in to meet them, they talked about problem men as if they were an everyday downside of the job, like some of my mates complain about commuting or long hours in the office.

Running a brothel in Russia can lead to serious jail time, which is a major disincentive to would-be pimps, so these girls were working as a collective without a pimp. They all chipped in for the flat rental and security and kept the rest of their earnings themselves. It was a good system on the face of it, but the conditions they were working in were rancid. They were seeing up to ten guys a night, having sex in dingy rooms with grimy bedsheets and still only earning around £70 in a shift.

Natalya, one of the girls I spoke to, told me that the job had got a lot harder since the financial crisis because there were more sex workers, fewer clients and prices had dropped as a result. As for it being safer than working on the streets, the girls could only afford one security guard per shift and sometimes had to deal with violent men turning up in gangs, carrying knives, knuckledusters and even guns, who beat and raped them, stole their money and cut up the guard. Like the prostitutes on the street, they were risking their lives every time they went to work.

'Can't the police help?' I asked Natalya.

'Come on, very funny!' she said with a wry chuckle, as if I was asking the dumbest question ever.

It could have been depressing having tea with these women and hearing their stories, but they were so brave and funny about what they were up against that I felt inspired. They were doing what they had to do to survive – and just getting on with it, relying on friendship and humour to get them through. I felt so much respect for them. Still, it made me angry to see how difficult and dangerous their conditions were.

Imagine going to work knowing you could easily be beaten up, stabbed, raped or even killed while you were there. You wouldn't go, would you? Not in a million years – unless you felt you literally had no alternative. So what's the answer? It seems to me that either the social conditions that drive women into prostitution have to get better, or their conditions at work need to improve. And men need to realise that violence against women is unacceptable in any situation.

Getting to know Natalya and other women who sell sex around the world has made me feel strongly that the laws on prostitution should change in the countries where it is illegal.

Every sex worker I've met wants it to be decriminalised. They don't want to be sneaking around, dodging the police, working in unsafe places, scared to go to the authorities if they've been battered, only to be told that they shouldn't have been there in the first place. They have all told me that if they had the law on their side, they would feel more confident about reporting abuse; they want to be treated in the same way that law-abiding citizens are.

It comes as a surprise to some people that I am fiercely pro legalisation, but I feel that if you give sex workers a safe, clean, warm brothel, with condoms, clean sheets, a buzzer that allows the guys in and out and security downstairs, then prostitution becomes a reasonable transaction. And that's all it is – a transaction. It will always exist, whether we like to admit it or not; it's ridiculous to think we're going to eradicate it. There will always be the appetite and there will always be people who are willing, so we have to make it as safe as possible, prevent assaults against prostitutes and hold abusive clients legally accountable for their actions. It's outrageous that men so often get away with sexual abuse and violence against sex workers, because either their crimes go unreported or they are not taken seriously by the authorities.

In a brothel with cameras and security, these guys aren't going to feel that they could batter or murder a woman as easily as they could as they could when they're down an alley with them. It's as straightforward as that. If the police took violence against prostitutes more seriously, and if sex workers felt more confident about reporting abuse, they would be stronger and safer. But until they get official status, they will continue to risk assault and exploitation because they don't have a legal leg to stand on.

I'm under no illusion that most prostitutes are happy with what they do. Many of them are terribly unhappy and don't want to be there. Still, in my opinion the only way to keep them safe – or as safe as you possibly can, given what they're doing – is to make prostitution legal.

Report after report shows that decriminalising prostitution makes the job safer and the workers less vulnerable. But, for me, the case for legalisation is never stronger than when you're sitting having a cuppa with a girl who tells you she's been raped and battered in the course of trying to earn a living.

It's not just the law – attitudes also need to change. In Turkey, sex work is legal, which I found surprising when I visited in 2016. At the same time, there's an overwhelming stigma attached to being a prostitute. Several of the girls I met said that their families would kill them if they knew what they were doing to earn money, even though it was legal.

Turkey felt quite confused at times. Sitting between east and west geographically, it doesn't know if it wants to be European and lean more to the liberal side of things or be part of the Middle East and more Islamic and conservative. Although modern Turkey was founded as a secular state with separate church and state, it can feel as if the conservative, religious government of President Erdoğan is blurring the boundaries. The climate is becoming more repressive and that's bad news for everyone. There is a deep divide between the Turkish people and they're fiercely loyal to the side they choose.

Attitudes to women in Turkish society are totally old school. A woman is generally expected to be a virgin until she is married. A wife is required to have sex with her husband whenever he wants it. She is not expected to be a sexual being or have her own desires. Oral sex is taboo for a lot of couples.

I met a guy outside a brothel who said that Turkish men's wives are too 'fat, ugly and old' to have sex with and won't do the sorts of things the men would like them to do, so for dirty, erotic, outlandish sex, their husbands go to prostitutes. Other guys I met tried to show me porn on their phones and offered me money to have sex with them. I saw a clear split in the way a lot of men view women – as respectable wives or prostitutes, and nothing in between. It all seemed pretty messed up.

But I guess if you condemn premarital sex, throw in a large helping of religious repression, allow state-run brothels, promote widespread disapproval of the LGBTQ community and add easy access to gay and straight internet porn, things are going to get complicated.

There was a big shift in the official attitude to prostitution underway in Turkey while I was there. The government had been denying licences to new sex workers for years, so a lot of brothels had shut down. There were 1,500 state-approved brothels remaining – and a mind-blowing 100,000 illegal brothels. Prostitution was being driven underground and becoming a lot more dangerous.

I visited one of the legal brothels and met Hulya, who was coerced into prostitution at the age of 15 and had been a sex worker for more than 20 years. She was really attractive – we couldn't show her face on camera because we didn't want to identify her, but she was very beautiful.

Hulya said with a weary air that she would rather do something else, but had no hope of ever getting out of prostitution. No one would employ an ex-hooker, and it would be impossible to erase her job history from her official ID papers. What kept her going was the thought that she was providing a service – and perhaps even saving lives. This was definitely a comfort to her.

'They say prostitution shouldn't exist,' she told me. 'But there is a need for it in this country. This is a place where people come to live out the sexual fantasies that they can't enact at home. Oral sex is often out of bounds between married couples; sex is taboo, sex education non-existent.'

In Turkey today, many women live in fear of male violence. For instance, if a bride is not clearly a virgin on her wedding night, she is at risk of being killed by the groom or a member of her family. There has to be blood the first time she has sex, otherwise she is in deep trouble.

Without sex education, there are many men who haven't a clue about what to do. Hulya had dealt with clients who tried to push their penises into her belly button, thinking that was the correct place to put it to have sex. It sounds so crazy, but it actually happens! Of course, if a man tried to do that to his bride, there wouldn't be any blood and he would think the worst, with potentially horrendous repercussions. By educating them, Hulya felt she was helping to prevent women being harmed.

I was astounded when she told me that she saw up to 50 clients a day and estimated that about a third of them wanted to act out paedophile fantasies. One particular guy wanted to call her by his daughter's name while they had sex. He was clearly mentally unwell, but in some warped way she felt she was helping out, because if he could relieve himself of his feelings by having sex with a prostitute, perhaps he wouldn't go on to abuse his daughter. Hulya made sure to protect the newer girls from the guys with serious psychological issues.

She looked after them and sent the younger clients to them, the ones who didn't have so much going on upstairs.

Hearing Hulya's story reaffirmed for me that if you don't spend time with prostitutes, it's all too easy to judge them from a distance. You can imagine that they are cut-throat and hardened and have no feelings, but so many of them are actually very maternal and supportive. 'Come on girls! We're in this together. I'll look after you and you look after me.' This was Hulya's attitude, and I admired her for it. It amazes me how people manage to stay positive in such difficult circumstances. I just can't imagine what it must be like for her having to deal with those men day to day.

Life was even tougher for the women selling sex on the streets of Istanbul, especially for the Syrian refugees with no state support. They did it simply in order to exist. Of all the women I met while I was investigating sex lives around the world, my heart went out to Yana, a lovely Syrian mum of three who was doing all she could to keep herself and her family afloat. She was a true survivor, a real trooper, and it was inspiring to spend time with her.

Yana was one of the three million Syrian refugees who had fled to Turkey since the outbreak of war. Before this, she had run a post office in Aleppo, but now she had to beg for a living. When she couldn't make enough to feed herself and buy medicine for her sick husband back in

Syria, her only other choice was to sell her body. She literally had nothing else to offer, apart from the clothes on her back.

Her hometown of Aleppo was among the cities worst hit by the civil war. It destroyed everything – her house, her business and her family, all torn apart by the chaos. She fled her home after it was bombed by Isis; nothing of her old life remained. She was still in touch with her husband, who had been too ill to flee with her, but her children had scattered and she wasn't sure if they were still alive, which was heartbreaking for her.

Eighteen months before I met her, she'd paid a trafficker to walk her across the border into Turkey and she was now living in a crumbling, filthy, rundown area of Istanbul, with no help or support from the Turkish government. In her previous life, she had been a contributing member of a functioning society, but war had pushed her to the outer limits of another country's system, where she was alone to fend for herself.

Yana was funny, tactile and had a great sense of humour – but when she came to tell me her story, she couldn't stop crying. She was wearing a scarf that hid most of her face while we spoke, but the pain in her eyes was there to see. She was still deeply traumatised. She was 35 but looked older.

Since her arrival, she told me, she had experienced a side of life that she'd never thought to see. 'There were days when we couldn't find a piece of bread to eat,' she said. 'I did bad things just to eat. If I didn't work, we would suffer.'

The going price for sex with a Syrian refugee was £1.25. Yana said she had often been insulted by the men who came to her. 'They say, "You're Syrian, fuck you,"' she sobbed, admitting that she had been raped and abused while in Turkey.

In Istanbul, Syrian refugees are seen as a nuisance, at best. You could sense the waves of bad feeling coming at us as Yana and I walked along the street together. People called her names and I got into an altercation with some men who racially abused her and refused to let her into a market. When things got heated, they sprayed something in our eyes, which really stung. I was shocked by how openly they showed their aggression.

Until she crossed the border, Yana had only ever been intimate with her husband, who now had no idea how she was making ends meet. 'He would kill me if he knew,' she said.

Now she was having sex with two or three men a night, something she clearly found disgusting and humiliating. She was at the other end of the spectrum from Avlora, the Russian call girl I met in Moscow. Her life and her choices were worlds away.

Yana was broke, she was dirty and she was embarrassed that she smelled, because she rarely had a chance to wash. At the same time, she just got on with it. Every day was a never-ending grind, but somehow Yana remained quite sassy and go-get-'em. She had been living a really bleak existence for a long time but in many respects she remained giggly and girly. She was inspirational because she had nothing and was still raring to go. Her attitude was, When you've been through hell and you're still standing, what is there to fear? The only thing that can happen is that you can die. And if you feel like your life has become relentless and harrowing anyway, perhaps you don't fear death in the same way that others do.

Her approach was typical of so many of the sex workers I've met, who have found themselves up against it, with no choice but to sell themselves to exist. 'I'm here and I've got to take charge,' she told me.

It's easy to have preconceived ideas about prostitution if you're a Western woman who doesn't sleep with men for money. But I think people would feel differently about sex workers if they sat down and had a conversation with them. Some women don't ever do a day's work in their lives, and that's fine – who am I to judge? – but I'd be really disappointed if these women judged prostitutes, who are doing whatever they can to get by, often in very difficult circumstances.

I, for one, have so much respect for them.

7

Babs, Derya and Tiera

Trans prostitution

Babs was amazing. She was my girl. She was so, so warm and lovely. As we walked along the street, she'd clasp my hand and kiss me and say, 'Oh, my Stacey!'

She was larger than life, bubbling with vitality, typically Latin; a huge character with deep, soulful eyes and a dazzling smile. I really liked her and felt sure we'd be pals if I lived in Rio de Janeiro, her hometown. And her family were so sweet – her nan, all her pals. It was great to hang out with them.

'Stacey! Come and sit down! Have some food with us,' they'd say. They were so friendly and welcoming.

Babs was a top performer at the Rio Carnival, a total star. She was the first transgender woman ever to lead the parade, which is a massive deal in a country where people spend all year long looking forward to Carnival. Wow. You literally cannot overestimate what a privilege and an honour it was for her to fill that role.

It was like a fairytale. When the cameras were on Babs and her image was being beamed to tens of millions of people around the world, she was celebrated for being a beautiful and talented performer. She was the face and body of a liberal, accepting culture. She was the star of the show, the queen of samba, right up there with the rest of Brazil's top celebs. She was an inspiration.

But everything changed as soon as the dust settled on Carnival season.

One minute she was up on a pedestal and her life was all sequins, glitz and glamour as she led the parade at the Sambadrome, the next she dropped out of the sky and landed with a bump on the streets, where she struggled to earn her living as a prostitute. Overnight she went from celebrity to social down-and-out.

The contrast felt really stark: during carnival she was centre stage, respected, admired and adored; the rest of the time she was on the side of the street running the risk of being killed. It was a dramatic fall from grace and understandably confusing for her. She couldn't help asking why society had such double standards, especially as many of the cisgendered star performers at Carnival had lucrative jobs as actors, models and entertainers during the rest of the year.

Babs longed to give up prostitution. Unlike Alvora in Russia, she truly despised it. She loathed being on the streets – there was no part of her that enjoyed being a sex worker. But when times were hard, it was her only way of paying bills and supporting her nan.

It feels like the world is waking up to the vast numbers of people whose gender identity doesn't match their birth-assigned sex, as well as the idea that gender can vary beyond simply being male or female. But life as a trans person remains incredibly challenging, even in countries like Brazil that have a history of tolerance and liberalism. Babs was a perfect example of how discrimination against transgender people can affect their ability to get jobs and earn money. A trained dancer, she desperately wanted to spend the rest of her year doing anything other than sex work – she would have been so much happier cleaning or working in a shop – but prejudice against trans people constantly pushes them into underground economies like prostitution and drug dealing. Most of the trans people I've spent time with over the years have been sex workers. And, like most of the prostitutes I've met, they had a tough time earning their keep.

As many as three-quarters of all reported murders of trans people in the last few years were in Central and South America, where the life expectancy of trans women is just over 40.

'It's scary, Stacey,' Babs said. 'I never know whether I will make it home alive. But if we don't have enough to eat at home or we haven't paid a bill I'll go because it's the only choice I have.'

Brazil is considered forward thinking when it comes to LGBT rights, despite its machismo culture and a growing population of hardline evangelists. There are legal measures to combat hate crimes and there are widespread anti-discrimination laws. Since 2011, transgender people have been allowed to change their names and sex on their identity documents; they can also join the military. But members of the LGBT community are worried by recent signs of a wave of conservatism sweeping across the country, including a furious public debate about whether homosexuality is a 'disease' that can be 'cured' with gay 'conversion therapy'.

Trans people especially face a huge amount of prejudice, particularly in the workplace. Very few openly trans people are doctors, lawyers or IT professionals in Brazil. Only a tiny percentage have a university education. They are far more likely to do informal work like cleaning, hair and beauty, working in nightclubs or prostitution.

It's almost impossible to smash the stereotype, Babs told me. 'If someone sees a trans woman, they're already thinking, even if she's not a sex worker, that she should be doing sex work, because it's a label we've been given,' she said.

'I once asked a friend if I could be a cleaning assistant, cleaning the floors. He laughed at me and said, "Barbara, you don't look like a cleaner." And I said, "I need to work." We want social equality.'

Like Babs, many of Brazil's visible trans population were assigned male at birth and identify as women. Some undergo the process of transition and live as the gender they identify with, as she has done. Others – but by no means all – go further by taking hormones and having surgery. The country's health service provides free gender reassignment surgery for about 100 people a year, according to the Ministry of Health of Brazil, although many more have operations in private clinics. None of the girls I got to know had opted for it, though.

Babs was a woman but kept her penis because it meant she could give or receive, whereas once you take the dick away, you can only receive. With a dick, you've got more tools in your belt, so to speak – especially as a sex worker. It attracts men who aren't openly gay and can pretend to themselves that they're having sex with a woman.

'But in an ideal world, what would you do?' I asked her.

'Oh, Stacey!' she sighed.

A person's transition process is very personal, so I didn't push it, but I got the impression that she hadn't made up her mind yet. Sometimes she longed to feel totally like a woman, but she also liked the sensation of having sex – and I don't think it's as good after surgery.

Babs's most important dilemma right then was how to get off the streets, though. She felt she deserved better, and so did the other girls forced out there with her. I could feel the tension in the air when I went out with her and some of the other girls.

According to one charity fighting for trans rights and recognition, 144 transgender people were murdered in Brazil in 2016, the year I got to know Babs. That's nearly three trans people turning up dead every week. And a lot of LGBT activists say that many other assaults and killings probably went unreported, because of stigma or fear of the police, so the figures could be far higher. It's shocking and unacceptable.

There are numerous cases of the police attacking and killing trans people, especially in the more remote areas of the country, where the prejudice tends to be at its worst. Even in Rio, they're not rushing to protect them when they get into trouble. I hung out with Babs and the other girls in a well-known spot next to some hot-dog stands, where I definitely got the sense that the hot-dog guys kept an eye out for them. It's a sad fact that in an emergency, the police would probably respond to the guys quicker than they would to the girls themselves, so they took it upon themselves to look after them.

It was quite a sweet set-up. One guy was obviously attracted to trans girls, but he had a girlfriend and was trying to play it down. His pal was noising him up though, saying, 'You've shagged all of the girls who come here!'

'No, I haven't!'

'Yes, you have.'

It was laddy humour, but they weren't disrespectful or unkind, and it offered a bit of light relief for Babs and the others as they tried to earn enough to make it worthwhile being out until dawn. There was a strong friendship among the girls too, and they all looked out for each other. They were amazing – I don't know how they managed to stay upbeat, but they kept on smiling and joking.

But every night was full of frustration for Babs. The danger made her nervous and she constantly worried that she wouldn't earn enough to pay the bills, or provide for her nan. It was a horrible situation, and very unpredictable. At one point she walked down an alley with a guy who then decided he wanted to take cocaine with her. She turned him down and walked away trembling, hoping he wouldn't get nasty. He didn't but of course she didn't get any money from him, either.

I really felt for her. She and her nan lived in a basic apartment in a rundown area of Rio, but she always managed to emerge from her home looking totally fabulous and smiling. It was sad to see such a talented, big-hearted woman – a Carnival superstar – selling her body against her will and scrabbling around to pay the bills because society didn't treat her equally.

Social stigma is probably the biggest obstacle for trans people as they try to get on with their lives. It's a massive problem in Turkey – although Istanbul has a dynamic LGBT community, gays, lesbians and trans people don't have the legal status or protection available in Brazil, and Turkish society is far more disapproving. While I was there in 2015, the government's crackdown on prostitution was in full force and LGBT rights, such as they existed, were being squeezed.

It wasn't always this way. Unlike in other parts of the Muslim world, being gay is totally legal in Turkey – and has been since 1838, far longer than in the UK (more than a century longer, in fact). In 2003, the first gay pride march in a majority Muslim country went ahead in Istanbul and the trans community joined in the celebrations. It was a massive breakthrough and in the years that followed the march grew in size and visibility, attracting tens of thousands of people.

Then in 2015, a year after Erdoğan went from being the Turkish PM to being President, the authorities withdrew permission for the march. They used water cannon and rubber bullets to break up the crowds that defied the ban. The march was outlawed the following year and again in 2017. Understandably, the LGBT community began to lose hope of gaining the legal protections they had been campaigning for, including stronger anti-discrimination laws. As it was, they were facing ever-worse social stigma under the increasingly repressive government.

Although it's legal to be gay and trans, it's not easy to be open about it in everyday life. One activist I got to know told me that there's a lot of fear in the community, partly because hate crimes against gay and trans people are not taken seriously by the police. He knew of trans prostitutes who had been murdered, their bodies dismembered and silicon breasts sliced off – and when these crimes were reported on the news, officials dismissed them by saying the victims shouldn't have been sex workers if they wanted to go on living. In other words, they brought about their own deaths; they practically murdered themselves. Case closed. End of.

It showed such a lack of respect for these women. It was almost encouraging their clients to think, I can do what I like, because she's a trans prostitute. What are the authorities going to do?

Yet like Babs and the other girls in Rio, the trans women I spent time with in Turkey tried to make the best of things and come out laughing. Things were so difficult politically and socially there that I wonder if they were thinking, We've just got to have a laugh and get on with things.

Derya, one of the girls I got to know in Istanbul, definitely had this attitude. She was very obviously a woman who had been born in the wrong body, with a strong maternal streak and a giggly girly side. She acted as if she was onstage all of the time: very charismatic and showy, she never switched off. She was good fun and could also be really bossy.

I arranged to meet her in a café before she went on a political march. Turkey was having an election and the secular CH Party was trying to mobilise as many voters as possible to defeat Erdoğan, who was planning to extend his powers if he got in. Derya was one of the thousands turning up to demonstrate their opposition to him.

I was having a cup of tea with the film crew, wondering where Derya had got to, when she came through the door and said indignantly, 'It's freezing! Where have you been? You took so long!'

'We've been waiting for you!' I protested.

'Oh, girl, I had to go to the toilet,' she said. It turned out that she'd had to wash her hands because she'd been with a guy.

We sat down for a cup of tea. Halfway through, she got a call. 'Shit, we're going to have to go right now!' she said.

'But we've got a sequence to film around the march,' I said.

'No, just come back to mine!' she insisted.

Derya worked as a prostitute on the streets and through her own website. Her life was pretty chaotic – she had to take the jobs whenever they came up, film crew or no film crew. She was lucky she had her own little house. It was simple and quite cold, but it was hers.

Just after we got there, her client turned up. I went into the sitting room and hid. The television was on loud – Derya always made sure it was turned up enough for her clients to hear, so that they would assume someone else was in the house. It reminded me of how dangerous it is to invite a stranger into your home when you're alone, and how scary. I know I'd be petrified.

I heard a growl from the bedroom. Suddenly it felt like I was back at school – you know, when you're at a house party and you can hear your mate shagging a guy? Honestly, I just wanted the floor to open up and swallow me! To make things worse, there was a budgie in a cage next to me and the budgie went nuts every time the guy growled. Something bubbled up inside me and I couldn't stop giggling. It was awful.

'This is serious, Stacey,' the director said, trying to say the right thing even though we were both really laughing.

It went on for ages and I really felt for Derya having to work so hard to get rid of him. After he had gone, she showed us her hands, which were raw and throbbing from jerking him off for so long. She had quite big hands because she'd been born in a male body and I thought, How many times have you had to go up and down his dick for them to be so sore?

In the end, she'd told him to get on with it. He finally came by touching and sucking her penis, her biggest asset as a trans sex worker.

'They never admit to being gay, but about 70 per cent don't get an erection until they suck or touch my dick,' she said.

More than two-thirds of her customers were guys who were struggling with their sexuality, because conservative society said it was wrong to be gay, even though it was legal. And they convinced themselves that they weren't gay because they were having sex with someone that looked like a woman, even though she still had a penis.

It was really messed up. There was a muddle of psychological, cultural and social factors at war in the minds of so many of the men I met in Turkey. A group of guys I talked to outside a trans brothel in Istanbul wouldn't accept that sleeping with a trans female was a gay thing. They insisted they were 'normal' and told me that trans prostitutes were popular because they were more 'hardcore' than other prostitutes. They started showing me photos of anal sex on their phone to demonstrate their point. I was interested in what they had to say, but glad to get away.

We finally made it to the political march, where Derya sang and chanted and waved flags in support of the CHP along with thousands of other people who didn't want an Islamic government. Derya expressed real worry about the way things were going. 'In Turkey today, homosexuals are being killed,' she said. 'This is not a good time. Attacks against us will increase if Erdoğan gets in again.'

She was gutted when Erdoğan won the election. Many of the people I spoke to felt like Turkey had taken a huge step backwards. They knew that just getting back to where they were before the election was going to take a massive struggle, let alone winning any new freedoms.

All across the world, trans people from all walks of life, racial and ethnic backgrounds are fighting for rights that others take for granted – at home, in the workplace, socially and medically. There are legal complications everywhere you look and a wall of false assumptions blocking them. People who don't know enough about trans issues assume that trans people are mixed up, delusional, crazy, promiscuous, gender fluid, bisexual … the list goes on. It's totally unfair. You can't jump to conclusions about trans people any more than you do about anyone else.

Even in America, where actress Laverne Cox featured on the cover of *Time* magazine in mid-2014 and Caitlyn Jenner was *Vanity Fair*'s cover girl the following year, it feels like there's still a long way to go. Many US states insist that if someone who wants to be legally recognised for the gender they identify with – rather than the sex they were born into – they must have sex reassignment surgery, even if that person doesn't feel it is necessary to their transition. Some states exclude transgender people from their hate-crimes legislation and some have no hate-crimes legislation at all. So America can be a very dangerous place for trans people to live and work.

One of the first things Trump did as president was to abolish transgender students' rights to use the bathrooms corresponding with their gender identity. Five months after that, he reversed Obama's plan to allow openly trans people to work in the military. It's anyone's guess how far he will try to push back the advances already made by the transgender community. The Laverne Fox issue of *Time* said that the battle for transgender rights and recognition was the new civil rights frontier. High profile trans trailblazers like Laverne, Caitlyn and Chelsea Manning, along with activists working at all levels, from local to government, are making sure it stays in the headlines.

While I was in Detroit in 2014 filming a programme about homelessness, I met Tiera, a 26-year-old trans woman who had been living and working as a prostitute on the streets of Detroit for over six years, with very little social or welfare support. It seems amazing to me that in the richest and the most privileged country in the world, Tiera's situation was every bit as bad as Babs's in Brazil and Derya's in Turkey. Worse, actually, because she was homeless.

Tiera had been in and out of foster care as a child. She'd identified as female since she was 14 and I think she would have liked to have the op, but years of feeling afraid that her family wouldn't accept her for who she truly was had led her to live a secret life and fend for herself on the streets. It's a familiar story. Almost half of all homeless young people in America identify as lesbian, gay, bi or transgender. Many of them have been rejected by their families because of their sexual orientation or gender dysphoria.

Tiera was in a bad place in more ways than one. Her hometown of Detroit, once one of the richest cities in the US, went bankrupt in 2013. The city's troubles date back to the civil turbulence of the late 1960s, when thousands of families moved away from the urban centres in the so-called 'white flight', leaving behind mainly poor Latino and black families. The job market collapsed, the infrastructure crumbled and now the city doesn't generate enough wealth to support the remaining population. There are 20,000 homeless people on the streets and no money to help them get back on their feet. If you're homeless in Detroit, you have a higher risk of dying on the streets than in any other American city.

I arrived there during the coldest winter the city had seen in 20 years – the worst possible time to find yourself living rough. The city was freezing cold and eerily deserted; it felt like a ghost town in some areas. Nearly a third of all the properties in Detroit were unoccupied – around 70,000, including hospitals. I saw rows and rows of houses – sometimes whole streets – sitting there totally empty.

You would think that all these vacant houses would offer a solution to the huge numbers of homeless people, but it wasn't that simple, especially not for Tiera and the other sex workers. People didn't want prostitutes in their streets, because with them came customers, drugs and unwelcome chaos. So the neighbours sometimes set the empty houses on fire so that no one could sleep there and they wouldn't have to deal with all the crazy shenanigans. The fires could be fatal if there were people asleep inside, so the squatters had to be constantly alert and ready to escape at the first smell of smoke. It was an exhausting way to live.

Yet the alternative was worse, as it was hard to imagine anyone surviving outside at minus 20 degrees. People were losing the tops of their ears and fingers to frostbite. I worried about Tiera sleeping out at that temperature. At the end of a day's filming, I'd think, I hope she's still here tomorrow. The cold was unbelievable; it was so, so painful and biting that we had to wear layers and layers of clothes just to go out filming for an hour. It got so cold that you couldn't think. I had hand warmers in every pocket and down my shoes. The camera kept stopping and starting and we tried to keep it warm by taping hand warmers round it, which helped a bit. Every 15 minutes we had to get back in the car and stick it in front of the heat.

I visited a centre that offered support to Detroit's homeless, but it only provided chairs, not beds.

'I know that sounds really cruel, as if we've no sympathy,' one of the staff told me, 'but if we make it too comfy here for them, there's no drive for them to get themselves sorted.'

There were other shelters that housed people for a couple of nights, but after that they were forced to move on and find somewhere else. Again, the idea was not to make them too comfortable, so there was still that fire in them to find something more stable and long term. It seemed pretty harsh treatment in the dead of winter. When you are chilled to your bones, it's almost impossible to keep any kind of fire going inside you.

Tiera didn't stay in shelters because, as a trans woman who hadn't been through gender reassignment surgery, the law required her to be housed with the men. Like a lot of homeless trans women and gay lads, she didn't feel safe there. At the very least, she would be risking verbal abuse. People are still so judgemental that it was more hassle than it was worth.

Tiera preferred to take her chances by hopping through windows into empty houses. I went with her when she broke into a vacant family home that she had slept in before, where she was amazed to find her blanket still in the cupboard room where she had left it, but not at all surprised to see six used condoms on the floor, left behind by other squatters. It was really weird going in there, really scary, especially as a couple of nights earlier she had been chased out of an abandoned building by a guy pointing a pistol at her. And it didn't feel any warmer inside the house than outside in the snow, either.

When she didn't have any luck finding a building to sleep in, Tiera often spent the whole night working and then caught up on her sleep during the day, at a friend's house. She had a good pal called Julisa who was constantly worried about her safety and tried to look out for her as much as she could. Julisa would wait with Tiera for her 'dates' near the laundromat on Six Mile and Woodward, where a lot of the girls worked. Whenever Tiera got into a car, Julisa took down the number plate. Then she'd go home and wait for Tiera to call or show up 20 or 30 minutes later. It was a sweet friendship.

Julisa was pretty and feminine and was able to earn money in a way that Tiera wasn't, by doing photo shoots and bits and bobs. She went on *Jerry Springer* – things like that. She was a bit more put together because she had a home, even though it was tiny and very basic. I met her dad, who was very affectionate and greeted Julisa by saying, 'Hi, my little girl!' He didn't seem to have any issues with the fact that she had transitioned.

But Tiera didn't have the same kind of support, and the options open to Julisa weren't open to her, because she didn't look like a woman at all. She was very big and close up looked very masculine; it was very obvious that she had been born a man and so people teased her more than they would tease some of the other girls who had more money to make themselves look and feel how they wanted to. When I had a heart-to-heart with her, she told me that she was really embarrassed about the way she looked and the fact that she went to a bar and somebody said, 'You stink,' because she hadn't been able to shower that day.

It also made it harder for her to work, because a lot of the guys wanted girls who looked more feminine. But although she faced fierce competition on Six Mile and Woodward, it was also somewhere she could truly be herself because there were so many other trans women living and working there. However, it was still a really dangerous place to work.

Although Tiera was massive, she instantly seemed vulnerable when she got into a stranger's car, even though she ran about with a knife and a Taser and swore she wasn't scared.

'I'll slice him up if he tries not to pay me,' she'd say. 'I've got long arms, so I can just reach over and stab him.'

She stowed her knife in her handbag. 'I don't think there's a transgender woman in Detroit that doesn't carry a knife, a blade, some kind of Mace,' she told me. 'You have to. You risk being robbed. You risk the police not taking you seriously. And then we have to worry about all the brutalisation that goes on Six Mile and Woodward. Girls have lost their lives out here and I'm not ready to be one of those. A lot of the cases haven't been solved, which is sad. We've had girls that have been shot in abandoned houses, or their throats have been slit. There was one that had been dismembered, body parts found in different parts of Detroit. It's just not a safe environment for anybody, let alone being transgender.'

At least four trans women had been murdered in the previous few years. The violence wasn't anything like at Brazilian levels, but the fear was ever-present.

While we were waiting for Tiera to come back from one of her dates, Julisa started to worry. But she didn't want to call Tiera.

'I don't like calling her because I don't want her phone to ring and let her date know she has a phone and try to rob her.'

It felt like there was danger everywhere for Tiera and the other girls working the streets around Six Mile and Woodward. But despite all of this, despite all the difficulties, Tiera constantly found comedy and humour in her experiences, just like Babs and Derya. Tiera and Julisa were real troopers. They were very funny even though their lives were so dark. I'll never forget them punching the air and singing their own version of the Beyoncé song to me down the street, 'Who run the world? Trannies do!'

When you're spending time with these people it's tempting to be very earnest and straight and serious, in case you offend them. But actually I think they really appreciate it when you take the piss with them and you're on good form and show that you've got a sense of humour.

But near the end of filming I remember asking Julisa, 'What do you want? What do you hope for?'

And she said, 'I just want to be loved. I want a man who respects me and loves me and doesn't tease me.'

For Tiera, too, her biggest worry was that she would end up alone, unloved. 'I want someone that's going to love me for who I am, regardless,' she told me sadly.

I left Detroit hoping that she would find a way to turn her life around and earn her living without risking her life every time she went out to work. I was under no illusions that it would be easy, though. Social attitudes need to change massively before transgender people start getting the same treatment and respect as everybody else. Things will improve if more job opportunities are available to them – although this was complicated further by the economic situation in Detroit, as the city itself is trying to pick itself up and start rebuilding. But it wasn't going to happen overnight – and in the meantime, I could only hope that Tiera and others like her went on surviving their dangerous, chaotic lives.

Although attitudes to transgender people seem to be improving, it sometimes it feels as if equality is a long way off. So I was thrilled when I heard that Babs is cleaning now. My favourite girl found herself a little cleaning job and has been able to give up sleeping with people for money. Yaaay!

8

Sylvia

Abortion

'Are you OK?' the doctor asked.

It was incredibly hot. The air was filled with a strong, sickly smell. There was blood everywhere. I'm going to faint, I thought.

But I couldn't faint. I was in a delivery room holding the hand of a 13-year-old girl while she gave birth, stroking her head and trying to comfort her. She had no one else with her; I needed to fix up and stop being such a wimp.

There was just a thin sheet separating us from the surgeon who was performing the C-section on her. I could hear slippery, sucking sounds. The smell was overpowering.

Don't look anywhere other than her face! I told myself. Otherwise you're going to go over.

Thirteen-year-old Sylvia was one of the 50,000 teenage mums who give birth every year in Honduras, where abortion and contraception have been illegal since 2009. I'd met her by chance earlier in a pregnancy clinic where I was trying to find out about the effects of the ban. Later on, I was invited into the maternity ward. I'm not sure what I was expecting, but I wasn't prepared for the sight of a row of teenage girls squeezing out their babies side by side right in front of me. There were girls giving birth everywhere I looked.

At one point I opened a door and saw a woman with her legs wide open and blood gushing from her fanny.

Oh my God, I'm going to be sick! I thought. This is so mortifying.

I wasn't expecting to keep Sylvia company while she had her baby, either – I was called in at the last minute after she was rushed off for emergency surgery. It felt so surreal to see this terrified child lying on a bed having a child. Girls her age often aren't physically developed enough to give birth unassisted and they're five times more likely to die of complications than adult women. Her baby was two months premature and had to be put in an incubator.

Sylvia was one of the many casualties of the chaos and conflict I saw in Honduras while I was there to investigate femicide and violence against women in 2015. Lacking any sort of support network after she lost her parents, she moved in with her boyfriend at the age of 11. Now she was pregnant at 13 and totally dependent on a man. The fact that I was in the delivery room with her shows you how lonely she must have been, because she'd only met me that day. Like so many girls in Honduras, she was caught in a vicious cycle with no way out. It was clear that the future was going to be really difficult for her.

I had never witnessed life beginning before. It was momentous. Yet the circumstances surrounding this birth were so desperate and so painful that I couldn't help thinking it would have been better if Sylvia hadn't got pregnant. Then I saw her daughter. She was such a pretty little thing. I thought, Statistically and realistically, you are going to have a very difficult upbringing, but you are a precious baby!

Do you celebrate or commiserate in that situation? It's really tough. Sylvia seemed so small and scared. Since the idea of having a baby – at 28 – frightened the life out of me, even though I had a solid support network back in the UK, I couldn't imagine how petrifying it would be for her.

Another girl I met in the clinic that day, Sofía, had been raped and made pregnant by a family friend while she was babysitting to help her mum with bills. She didn't tell anyone what had happened for five months because she was so traumatised. When the truth came out, she had to drop out of school and give up her dreams of getting a good job, which was her only route out of poverty.

It wasn't an unusual case – a lot of teenage pregnancies in Honduras are the result of rape – but if Sofía had been caught trying to get the morning-after pill or have an abortion, she could have gone to prison for six years. In Honduras, as in most other South and Central American countries, it is a crime to interfere with God's reproductive plans. But statistically the guy who raped her would have got off scot free, because the political will to punish men for crimes against women just isn't there. Amazing, isn't it? The pressure that the Catholic church puts on the government to outlaw women's rights over their own bodies ensures that the girls and women of Honduras remain powerless. They are instantly under suspicion and risk being prosecuted even when they miscarry naturally.

The idea that these girls don't have a choice about whether they have a child really angers me. I am absolutely of the mind that it should be a woman's choice whether or not she wants to continue with an unplanned pregnancy. It is her body and her life; it should be her choice and only hers.

One night at 3am, I went out with a group of masked females putting up campaigning posters around town. In the dead of night, they could have been targeted by any number of hostile factions, from gangs to militia and police. But the risk was worth it to get their message across: 'We should have the right to choose what we do with our own bodies,' the posters said.

Who can rationally argue with that?

It's not just a problem in Honduras; women's bodies are a battleground all over the world. About 25 to 30 per cent of women worldwide live in countries with highly restrictive abortion laws. In places like Malta, Nicaragua and the Dominican Republic it is totally illegal to have an abortion under any circumstances – even if the mother is in danger of dying. And it is severely limited in many other countries.

In 2015, Amnesty International condemned a court judgement in Paraguay that denied an abortion to a ten-year-old who had been raped and made pregnant by her stepfather. A spokesman for Amnesty said that, 'forcing this young girl to continue with an unwanted pregnancy is tantamount to torture'.

What was the judge thinking? The girl was practically a baby herself.

Ironically, abortion rates are similar in countries where it is legal and where it is not, according to a World Health Organization study published a decade ago. You only need to look to the Philippines for an example. Abortion is illegal there, but it's estimated that 600,000 abortions are performed every year, often self-administered. Clearly, outlawing abortion does not deter women from seeking to end unplanned pregnancies. What it does affect is how safe the procedure is likely to be.

All over the world women are dying from botched abortions. In the Philippines alone, three women a day die from complications arising from abortion. They are swallowing toxic herbs, drinking poisonous teas, buying dodgy pills online, getting mates to kick them in the belly, inserting coat hangers into their wombs, going to inept abortion providers and throwing themselves down the stairs to try to halt their pregnancies. We could be talking about the nineteenth century, only we're not. This is happening now.

Millions of abortions that would be considered unsafe in the UK are performed elsewhere each year. As a result, there were tens of thousands of abortion-related deaths worldwide in 2014 – maybe as many as 40,000, according to some estimates, although it is of course impossible to know for sure. I just don't even know how to process that information. Nobody should be dying as a result of terminating a pregnancy. This is a human rights issue on so many levels.

The abortion debate often centres on people's different opinions about when life begins. Some say it's the moment of conception; others, like me, think it's the moment a child is born. Either way, if you're seeking to end an unplanned pregnancy, you're going to want to do it sooner rather than later. But even in countries like the UK, where abortion is legal and available, women face obstacles accessing early terminations.

Terminating a pregnancy became legal in the UK in 1967 (except in Northern Ireland, where it remains 'unlawful' unless the mother's life is at risk). But 50 years on, it is clear that the 1967 Abortion Act is completely outdated. As the UK law stands now, having an abortion is a criminal offence unless a pregnant mum is deemed by two doctors to need the abortion to protect her long-term mental or physical health. In practice, this is a formality, but it's still ridiculous and humiliating. Why can't a woman just say, 'I got pregnant by mistake and I would like to terminate the pregnancy'? But no, she has to say she might go mad if she doesn't have an abortion.

By far the most popular way to end a pregnancy in the UK is by medical termination, a non-surgical intervention using pills taken at intervals to induce miscarriage. But, according to Professor Lesley Regan, the head of the Royal College of Obstetricians and Gynaecologists, long delays in the NHS provision of abortions are causing some women to buy their pills over the internet. And under the Offences Against the Person Act 1861 (a law that was passed before women even had the vote!), a woman who takes a pill to terminate a pregnancy in the privacy of her own home can be punished by life imprisonment – and so can the doctor who gave her the pill.

It's totally crazy that a woman could get life for taking an abortion pill at home instead of in a clinic. Of course you need a degree of medical supervision, but under current legislation in England, the initial abortion pill must be taken inside a clinic or hospital and the woman must return to the clinic or hospital for further doses, risking the horrific possibility that she could start miscarrying on public transport. Activists are pressing hard for change, though, and at the time of writing,

Scotland was leading the way by allowing women to take the abortion pill at home, when clinically appropriate.

Attitudes are changing in England as well. Professor Regan has called for midwives to be allowed to administer abortion pills and for nurses and midwives to be permitted to start performing some terminations in the first 15 weeks of pregnancy to ease access to early abortion. And the British Medical Association, the biggest doctor's union, has called for the complete decriminalisation of abortion and for women to have access to terminations on demand without having to be approved by two doctors. Things are set to change after MPs won the right to introduce a bill decriminalising abortion back in March 2017, but it's hard to see why the law wasn't overhauled years ago. The fight for reproductive rights seems to be never ending.

Why is it such a battleground? I have always been fiercely pro-choice and I think I always will be but, just to make sure, in 2016 I spent two weeks in southern California at a summer camp run by a Christian pro-life group called Survivors. I wanted to see whether immersing myself in their world of anti-abortion activism could change my opinion at all. And boy, was it a learning experience.

Jeff White, the group's founder, is a legend among pro-lifers. I've heard that Jeff has been arrested more than a hundred times for his radical activism and done time in prison too. Survivors is famous for using graphic and gruesome imagery of aborted foetuses to get the pro-life message across in public places. I can imagine how this caused some legal troubles for Jeff. You're out doing your Saturday shopping with the kids and suddenly you're all staring at giant photos of dead foetuses? People are likely to complain, I'd say.

Jeff uses shock tactics to make people stop and think – and as I got to know him, I realised that he truly believed that what he was doing was right. He wasn't doing it out of spite or to rob women of their choice. He was doing it because he believed in his heart of hearts that we were murdering unborn babies. It was that simple.

I asked him, 'If that were true and I felt the same, I would be standing here with you. There is no way I would be justifying women killing kids. But I don't see it as a child. I see it as cells. And there are so many children here on earth *now* that need your help – why aren't you fighting for them?'

So we were coming from opposing planets.

Jeff called the group Survivors because one of his core beliefs is that anyone born after 1973, when abortion was made legal in the US, is a survivor of 'the American Abortion Holocaust' that supposedly followed. He claims that the number of 'children that we've murdered' since 1973 'makes Nazi Germany pale by comparison'. It's a controversial analogy that has pissed off many members of the Jewish community, and I completely understand them feeling that way. It's almost never relevant or helpful to use this term for anything other than the murder of the Jews by the Nazis. But I don't think Jeff minds offending people. In his view, making an impact is what matters, especially with the young people that he aims to attract to the cause.

Survivors is one of the only pro-life groups that trains high school kids and young people of college age to be anti-abortion activists. I arrived at the Survivors summer camp to find 50 people between the ages of 11 and 24 signed up to the course. They were there to learn about the horrors of abortion and how to argue, campaign and demonstrate against it. It seemed a bit of a strange way to spend a chunk of your summer holidays.

On our first day, we were given a welcome pack with our room allocation and other essential information. The next day, we plunged headlong into the emotive subject of abortion, photos and all. The first few days were really rough for me. It was hard being constantly told that abortion is murder – that there was no other way of looking at it. This is bollocks! I thought. Why have I come here? I was really angry.

But there was no escape – no going home to my life and my reality. I was totally embedded: I was eating with the campers; I was filming with them the entire day; I was even sharing a hotel room with a couple of them, because it was the only way to see what they were truly about. Spending the evenings with the girls and being there when they woke up first thing in the morning gave me a real insight into the way their minds were processing what they were learning.

There was a lot of crossover between the definitions of foetus and baby in the talks the camp leaders gave us, and a lot of opinions were presented as 'facts' or 'scientific facts'. At times, they sounded more like preachers than teachers, and as the days went on, they ramped up the emotion on the moral high ground. The kids kept being told that millions of babies would die if they didn't get out there and stop it happening. It was no wonder some of them looked like they had the weight of the world on their shoulders.

I asked a few of the girls if they would be prepared to die for the cause.

'Yeah, I would, I definitely would,' one of them said.

'I would, too,' another girl chipped in.

'Yeah, because it's basically giving your life for another 60 million human beings.'

'If it meant the end of abortion, like all legal abortion – all anything abortion – I would personally die, yeah.'

They were being totally sincere; they were experiencing all those big emotions that feel so raw when you're in your teens and early twenties. But I felt that sometimes Jeff played on their sensitivities too much.

After a few days of lessons, he took us all to a cemetery outside LA, where a memorial service was being held for 54 aborted foetuses that had been found nearby, 19 years earlier.

Shockingly, the foetuses had been dumped by the driver of the truck that was transporting them to a medical waste facility in 1997. They were found in boxes near the cemetery by a couple of young boys.

'Just think,' Jeff was saying, over sad keyboard music, 'if one of those children could have escaped that horrible death, they might be standing right here with you today. That's how old they are. And it is my prayer today that this will touch your heart and that you will say, no. No. Not now, not ever. Not on my watch.'

Now, I'm not saying that the dumping of aborted foetuses isn't appalling and wrong, because it is. But gathering a load of impressionable youngsters around a grave and playing them sad music while talking to them about innocent children dying could be seen as a little bit manipulative, I think. I mean, they're going to respond, aren't they? A lot of the kids were in tears – they were devastated by the thought of these dead 'babies', and couldn't understand how anybody could be cruel enough to do such a thing. I felt sorry for them; Jeff's teachings were so biased that he left them no room to make their own minds up.

'I know you think what you're doing is absolutely right,' I said to him, 'but what I find difficult to stomach is that you are targeting youngsters specifically because they're easier to manipulate. Why aren't you taking more adults on this course?'

'Because young people are enthused,' he replied. 'They can make real change and they're the future. They're the next generation coming up.'

'I think it's because they're easier to manipulate and mould to what you want them to be,' I said.

The remembrance service got everyone fired up and it wasn't long before we were out on our first street demonstration, using signs emblazoned with highly graphic images. But before we went, I had to say that I didn't feel comfortable going out there holding a sign, which didn't go down well with Jeff and some of the campers. Still, I just couldn't bring myself to do it.

We went out to Huntingdon Beach, which is famous for being pretty cool and laid back, and I found it really hard to support the demonstration. When I got talking to a guy who said he was pro-choice, it upset some of the campers even more. They couldn't get their head around the fact that I wasn't with them, because to them it was so straightforward and true. 'But she's so nice!' they'd say. 'Why does she approve of killing babies?'

There was a handsome young lad there called Andreas who couldn't understand why I didn't get it. 'I give up on her,' he said to my director one day. 'She's a lost cause, because she's just not listening and doesn't believe in what we do.'

I felt bad. I was in a really hard space, because I was slowly beginning to get pally with some of the campers. They were decent human beings and I liked a lot of them, but we weren't about the same things, so it wasn't easy. In fact, it was a really rough ride. Because they'd been fed these lines, they believed that abortion is a horrific crime. I can see how at a young age you would come to that conclusion, but life is so much more complicated than that. When you're a woman you realise that it should always be the woman's choice first and foremost. It's not OK to be dictated to in 2018.

Still, for me it was a lesson learned that you shouldn't just surround yourself with people who have similar political and social views – you should challenge yourself and make sure that you really do believe what you say you believe. Because when you spend so much time with people you like but disagree with, it makes you think. It's very difficult to stick to your guns when you have 30 or 40 people around you who are adamant that you're wrong and they are right. You do question if you've got it wrong. It makes you think about the woman that you want to be, which is healthy. It's a good thing.

I tried role playing my way through the main pro-choice and pro-life arguments in a group session. One essential skill for any pro-lifer was how to respond to the argument about rape. What if a woman has been raped and becomes pregnant? Why should she be forced to keep the baby if she doesn't want to?

One of their lines was: 'Punish the man, don't punish the unborn child.' Another was: 'You were still raped. Abortion won't un-rape you.'

They just couldn't see it from the woman's point of view. I tried to explain why I had a problem with that. 'I have met women who have been raped and it was in countries where abortion is illegal,' I said. 'They were forced to go through with the pregnancy, and they killed themselves. They just couldn't look at that child.'

The campers were encouraged to offer women alternatives to abortion. 'Whatever the woman has been through, we will help her and give her the stability that she deserves,' they were schooled to say. 'The child will bring her joy. Or if she can't cope with the child, we'll give it to a family who can.' When they came up with idealistic solutions like this, I couldn't help thinking of 13 year-old Sylvia in Honduras and all the other teenage mums in her position. These sheltered American teens had such an uniformed view of the world. I appreciate that they were being sincere – but it was totally unrealistic. Just on a practical level: one in three women in the US has an abortion in her lifetime; there are millions of abortions worldwide every year. If they didn't happen, the planet would be even more densely populated than it already is. We would have so many more people here. There would be a lot more children suffering. There simply aren't enough families to 'give' millions of babies to. Social services would be bursting at the seams – and in some situations that's already the case. And women's rights and the struggle for equality would basically implode.

In my mind, it would be catastrophic.

In 2017, following their election losses, the Conservatives made a deal with Northern Ireland's Democratic Unionist Party (DUP). Suddenly the DUP were the most Googled party in Britain, because many people were alarmed by some of their policies. The DUP are anti-abortion, even though three in five people in Northern Ireland want it to be decriminalised for victims of rape and in cases where the baby wouldn't survive, according to a poll by Amnesty International.

I thought it was interesting that the party appeared to be at odds with the views of the Northern Irish electorate on such a fundamental human rights issue, despite being the biggest party in the province, but I was also wondering whether they could influence what happens in the rest of the UK, especially now that there are calls for a change in the law from the British Medical Association and the Royal College of Obstetricians and Gynaecologists. The DUP hold 10 seats in the House of Commons to the Conservatives 317, so while it's unlikely that they would hold the balance of power on the issue of decriminalising abortion when it gets debated in Parliament under this government, it remains a possibility. Could the DUP scupper decriminalisation of abortion in Northern Ireland and wider access to early abortion for women on the mainland? They are a political party. They have power, and that power has been seriously bolstered by the cheque for £1.5 billion Theresa May gave to the province in return for DUP support for her government.

I wanted to know more about them and interview key figures in the party so, a month after the UK election, I approached the DUP formally and informally to ask if they'd speak to me. I messaged one of their politicians and she came straight back to me, saying, 'Yes, in principle I have no dramas with meeting you, although we'd have to go through the press office …'

But then I followed up and got radio silence. She wouldn't speak to me. I'm just speculating, but I wonder whether they Googled me or had a look at Twitter and thought, Actually, we're probably not that interested in talking to her. Or perhaps she spoke to the press office and they just said. 'We're not doing it. We're not giving anyone any interviews.'

So I went to Northern Ireland to try and get inside the minds of DUP voters, enthusiasts and sympathisers instead. What was interesting was that a lot of them didn't necessarily agree with the party's socially conservative views on abortion and same sex marriage. For the party's Protestant, unionist supporters, it was more about keeping Irish nationalists Sinn Féin out. In a still-divided Northern Ireland, issues like abortion were less emotive than questions of loyalty to the party as a representative of their community. I realised that some people just went along with whatever DUP policy happened to be on abortion, even if they didn't particularly agree, because they supported them for other reasons. (I don't know if there was that same ambivalence among Sinn Féin supporters, but Sinn Féin's stance on abortion is very similar to the DUP's, and of course many Catholics are against both birth control and abortion – in theory, at least.)

Some DUP supporters felt more strongly than others, though. One young girl, Ruth, who had turned 19 about a week before we met, came from the DUP heartland; her father was involved with Ian Paisley Jr's election campaign and her entire family were staunch DUP supporters. It was slightly surreal talking to Ruth, because she was really sweet, innocent and kind in some ways, but when you got on to the subject of abortion she was fiercely adamant that she'd got this right and there was no room for manoeuvre. For her it was very simple and it was very straightforward: abortion was murder.

Ruth was deeply religious and I think her opinions were very much influenced by her beliefs and her interpretation of the teachings of the Bible. She is completely opposed to any change in the law on abortion or same sex marriage. Like the kids on the Survivors summer camp, she was prepared to go out on a limb and try and convince any woman who was even entertaining the idea of having an abortion that they were making the biggest mistake of their life. She said she would do everything within her power to make sure it didn't happen. She was against the idea of abortion in any circumstances.

To me, Ruth's views seemed idealistic, not realistic. 'Realistically, what can you do to convince a woman not to have an abortion if she wants one?' I asked her. 'Can you really swoop in, alleviate all of her concerns and make everything right?'

I disagreed with her, but I could see how genuine and sincere her opinions were. It's such an emotive subject and I sometimes think that people on both sides of the fence can be too intolerant. If you say you want tolerance you can't kick off when somebody has a different point of view. It's a very difficult balance to get right. And she was only young.

So what's the answer? There are fewer abortions in countries where women have easy access to contraception. In Eastern Europe, for instance, abortion rates have halved since the fall of Communism, when contraception became more freely available. Presidents and prime ministers who stand against abortion might bear that in mind.

But to the horror of women services providers around the world, on his first Monday in office as US president, Donald Trump signed an executive order to stop all US funding to NGOs that 'perform or actively promote abortion' anywhere in the world, even where abortion is legal. Every global health organisation that accepts US funding has to comply with this rule, known as 'the global gag' because it is a ban on even speaking about abortion. It includes NGOs providing HIV and malaria prevention services in remote rural villages and refugee camps, where it is easier said than done if they are also offering contraceptive services, or are partnered with big international providers of family planning like Marie Stopes, which performs terminations on behalf of the NHS in the UK – just that connection rules them out of receiving aid.

Activists around the world claimed that Trump's sweep of the pen would result in thousands of deaths from illegal abortions; further lost opportunities for girls and women whose schooldays and careers are cut short by pregnancy; children dying because their parents cannot afford to feed them; health clinic and outreach programme closures all over the world; fewer contraceptive services; even withdrawal of funding to help and counsel women traumatised by war and rape. I hope their predictions don't come true.

Since then, the Trump administration has also issued a ruling that makes it easier for US companies and insurers to opt out of providing free birth control to employees on the grounds of religious and moral beliefs, which will almost certainly increase the numbers of unwanted pregnancies – and abortions – in America.

At least there's hope that the old-fashioned UK abortion laws will be swept away. Hopefully, abortion will be decriminalised and available on demand, without the requirement of two doctors to approve every procedure or intervention, and the rules around medical terminations will be relaxed to allow people to have them at home, where appropriate. Meanwhile, MPs and councils are currently looking into ways of using antisocial behaviour legislation to stop people standing outside clinics harassing women going for abortions, trying to deny or coerce women out of their right to reproductive freedom. I'm hoping that new legislation will have passed through Parliament by the time you read this.

I often have conflicting feelings about some of the issues I look into, especially after seeing a different side of things when I meet the people who are affected by them. But in this case, I didn't change my mind, although I understand why the subject of abortion stirs up such strong emotions. I sympathise with the people who believe abortion is wrong, but I only have to think of 13-year-old Sylvia, too physically immature to give birth; Sofia, made pregnant by rape; the thousands of deaths a year that result from unsafe abortions; and the sheer numbers of terminations that take place every year, to know where I stand. Looking into this issue confirmed everything I thought I believed. It made me even more pro-choice than I was before.

9

Honoka-chan

Child sexualisation

Her name was Honoka-chan and she was ten years old. Or that was how old he imagined her to be. He kept her in his room and her role was to 'comfort' him – they often hugged and sometimes hugging led to sex. It aroused him to undress her, but she was hard to keep clean so he tended to ejaculate on her clothes, which he could take off and wash. When he penetrated her, he used a condom, for the same reason. He was in a relationship with what was basically a stuffed toy, but for him it was a real relationship.

It was really weird meeting him. I was in Japan looking into attitudes to child pornography and this self-confessed paedophile had agreed to speak to me about his sexual desires. He was very, very bizarre. He turned up at our hotel room carrying Honoka-chan in a cardboard box and, as he sat her on the bed and began to smooth down her clothes, I thought, I don't know if he's totally deluded or a guy who is genuinely attracted to children.

I was concerned because sometimes people will say that they're prepared to be interviewed, but when you meet them it's clear that they're not in a position to give real consent. You can interview them anyway, and afterwards, you can argue, 'Well, they gave us their consent.' But I really don't think this is fair to the vulnerable person who you have filmed, and it's something I would never do.

So we spoke to him for about half an hour off-camera in our hotel room and he actually turned out to be very articulate. He seemed clear in his views and thought processes, so I felt morally comfortable about filming him. I thought, This is a guy who says that he is attracted to children and that this doll stops him from acting that out. So yes, he is an important interviewee and somebody we should be giving time to on film.

Also, he was not an isolated lunatic; he wasn't the one nut job in Japan who really loves a doll. The child sex-doll industry there is booming, and I wanted to learn more about it.

I know of at least one factory in Japan churning out life-like child dolls with holes so you can have sex with them. There's so much demand for these dolls that they can't make enough of them. A lot of the time they are custom made: blonde or dark, with short hair or long, aged five or fifteen, wearing underwear or school uniform.

They can be happy-looking or have sad expressions on their plastic-moulded faces, because there are actually men out there who want to have sex with dolls that look sad. I was desperate to interview the factory manager, but he'd stopped giving interviews after an international backlash. I wanted to find out whether he thought child sex dolls might encourage paedophilia. Or did he think they could potentially save children from harm?

I wanted his point of view because I was back and forth in my mind. Is it better to allow these guys to make out with dolls, in the hope that it's enough for them and they never end up abusing real children? Or, is it inevitable that they'll get bored of a doll that doesn't move or respond and ultimately end up moving on to real children?

As yet, there have been no scientific studies carried out, so we don't know one way or another whether dolls could be a useful tool in the fight against child abuse. Are they a deterrent or an enabler? Is there a risk that the dolls will somehow validate their owners' feelings?

There is currently no known cure for paedophilia, medical or psychiatric, and treatments like cognitive therapy and taking drugs to kill the libido do not remove a paedophile's fundamental sexual attraction to children. It would probably be quite difficult to test whether sex dolls could provide a safe outlet for men who find children attractive, but I'm for anything that reduces the chances of children being harmed. We can't ignore the fact that walking, talking AI child sex dolls are just around the corner. Animatronic, AI-enabled, lifelike, silicon adult sex robots – or sexbots – are about to explode on the market, and the child versions won't be far behind.

It is currently illegal to import child sex dolls into the UK, although it is not against the law to own one. It's contradictory – obviously the law needs to be clearer. Between March 2016 and August 2017, 120 dolls were seized at UK border control points, with a judge ruling them 'obscene' in a landmark case. In a separate case, the first prosecution against a man who tried to import a one – through East Midlands Airport – was brought in 2016. When the police followed up, they found indecent images of children on his computer. In another case, a British man who tried to import a child sex doll from China was found to have thousands of pornographic photos of children between the ages of three and sixteen.

When I was in the Philippines I found out how much of a widespread, global problem child pornography actually is. I was in Japan to explore was why on earth anyone wants to look at these pictures. What do they get out of them? One of the many astonishing things about Japan is that it was legal to own child pornography until 2014. You couldn't produce, sell or distribute it, but you were fine to own it and watch it. Until 2014? It seems like madness.

I travelled there in 2016, two years after the law had changed, and I was curious to see whether it had made any difference to people's attitudes. On my first day in Tokyo, I was amazed by the huge number of sexualised images of children I saw across the city. They were everywhere you looked, from cartoon toddlers posing coyly in bikinis on enormous billboards to posters of flirty schoolgirls advertising household items.

On the day I was due to fly out of the UK, I couldn't stop throwing up. I was panicking, because I'd never, ever rung in sick to work and I felt really bad about it and Joyce, the director, was already out there, waiting for me. I managed to get there only a day late, which meant I literally got off the plane and went straight to film a sequence at a *chaku ero* shoot, which turned out to be a weird, surreal experience.

It's hard to describe *chaku ero* other than as child soft porn. It often involves photographing teenage girls dressed in school uniform, which is a huge fetish in Japan known as *joshi kosei* (meaning high school girl). But the models can be as young as toddlers. It's freaky. The models are never photographed fully naked and don't show their genitals, so it's not classed as child pornography, but it's clearly meant to be erotic, so how else can you define it? At the moment, it's a legal grey area, but in my mind it's pretty black and white.

Kazuko Ito, a Japanese human rights lawyer I spoke to, was in no doubt. '*Chaku ero* is child pornography. That's the reality,' she said.

At the shoot, a 19-year-old girl was being photographed suggestively in school uniform, little dresses and tiny white satin pants, with her hair in pigtails and ribbons. She was definitely legal – her body was totally developed and I believed that she was of age – but my issue was with the fact that they were desperate to make her look as young as humanly possible by dressing her up as a kid.

Even though I was tired, I managed to get a very telling interview with the director. He revealed that the youngest girl he had worked with was six years old. He had filmed her in a swimming costume, playing with toys.

'Her mum was standing behind the camera with her favourite doll, so that she would face the camera,' he said.

As far as he was concerned, there was no problem with filming young kids posing in swimming costumes, because it wasn't breaking the law. '*Chaku ero* doesn't show any nudity,' he said, sounding surprised when I asked if he was worried about encouraging paedophilia. 'If they're underage, they're clothed and there is no eroticism.'

'So why would middle-aged men want to look at them?'

He shrugged. To him it was simply business, and very lucrative at that. He made £35,500 from the six-year-old's shoot and £70,000 from a shoot with another very popular girl. But when I asked him if he would have been so relaxed about his 16-year-old daughter appearing in a similar shoot at the age of six, his face fell. 'It may sound extreme,' he said, 'but I would feel like killing her and then myself.'

It was hypocrisy at its most extreme. He completely separated himself and his own family from the girls he was photographing and exploiting. He saw them as commodities, not as human beings. It was creepy.

Chaku ero and explicit child abuse pornography are [illegible] two different things, but I wanted to know why there was even an appetite for *chaku ero*. 'How can you be prepared to try and mould these children into being sexual beings? How can you justify making a living off the back of that?' I asked.

He didn't have an answer.

Back at her NGO office, Kazuko Ito showed me more disturbing examples of *chaku ero*, including photographs of young girls wearing bikinis and swimming costumes, shot in provocative 'porn' poses. There was a ten-year-old lying back with her legs wide open, and what looked like a six-year-old in a thong that showed off her bum. Because these images weren't showing any breast area or genitals, they weren't officially classed as child pornography – although they clearly were.

I pointed to the six-year-old. Someone had brought her to the shoot – a mum, dad or family member. 'Why would they have allowed this to happen?' I asked.

Kazuko said that it was because they were so poor and had no other choice. It had been hard enough to accept this explanation in the Philippines, but in a rich country like Japan it didn't seem justified at all.

Kazuko was worried that the kids would be traumatised when they were older and realised what had happened to them. She called *chaku ero* 'a human rights violation' and was pressing for tougher laws around child pornography.

So what's behind Japan's problem with child exploitation? Both times I've been there it has been painfully apparent that there is this total obsession with youth. It's weird – I've never seen it anywhere else in the world and I've travelled extensively. In Japan, the younger you are, the more attractive you are, and they take it to ridiculous extremes. So by the time you're 25, you're ready for the dump. There's a saying about how no one wants Christmas cake after 25 December, and they call anyone over 25 'Christmas cake'.

In my mind, at 25 you're just coming into your own. I'm 30 now and I'm … just coming into my own. The older you get, the further you push it back: 40 is the new 30, 50 is the new 40, until suddenly you're just coming into your own at 50. But not in Japan.

Look, we all buy wrinkle cream; we all want to look younger than we are, we all want to look fresh. We want to hold on to our heyday years. But in Japan youth is fetishised, everything there is cute, cutie, cutesy. Cultural differences aren't bad or wrong, but you're entitled to question things, and I definitely find the whole schoolgirl fetish weird. *Joshi kosei*, also known as JK, is used to sell anything from used underwear to vacuum cleaners and cars. It is a brand that generates millions of dollars.

There's even a street in Tokyo called 'JK alley', where high school girls sell their time to passers-by. For a few yen men can hold hands, go for a walk or have a coffee with girls several decades younger than they are – and it's totally legit. The darker side of the business isn't apparent until you notice their minders in the background, or try to speak to the girls and ask them what other services they offer. I tried – and ended up being held against my will for two hours, after a couple of minder bullies called the police on me. It was a real eye-opener that the police sided with them even though I wasn't doing anything illegal.

Unbelievably, there are the 300 JK cafés across Japan, where adult men pay to spend time with underage girls who serve them alcohol. I don't know how that can be healthy in any society – but it is totally normal in Japan. I saw girls as young as 15 hanging out with middle-aged men in JK cafés, and the girls most in demand are the ones who flirt and talk about sex. In one café I went to, a guy could hang out with a girl for 40 minutes and drink unlimited booze for £35. How can it be acceptable for an adult man to get drunk and talk about sex to an underage girl?

In some places men can pay for 'walking dates', away from the café, where no one can monitor what happens. I spoke to a 17-year-old who worked in a café that offered walking dates. She said they were a cover for prostitution. 'They leave it to the customer and the girl to make an arrangement,' she explained.

'How many nights a week are you working there?' I asked.

'I have school, so I work two or three times a week,' she said, adding, 'Once you get popular, you might have sex with five to six men a day.'

So that was 10 to 18 men a week.

'As an "under", which is when you're under 18 years old, I get between 30,000 yen (£212) to 60,000 yen (£424) per man,' she went on.

'So they pay more because you're younger?' I asked.

'That's right. It is illegal, so under 18s cost more.'

On the surface, she seemed happy and confident with what she was doing, but later in our conversation she revealed that she suffered from depression and had been hospitalised for suicidal feelings.

'Girls in my line of work either have issues at home or are lonely,' she admitted. 'Of course, some do it to pay their school fees. I probably do it as a form of self-harm.'

When I visited an NGO drop-in centre and shelter for vulnerable high school girls, I was told that girls are sometimes assaulted, raped and kidnapped on walking dates. And while some girls said that working in a JK café is a harmless way to get a bit of pocket money, chatting and flirting with men, others told me their lives were shattered after they were coerced into paid sex.

Some of the JK girls are older and that's a different thing. My issue was with adult men paying to spend time with children. A law has since been passed prohibiting girls of 17 and younger from working in the JK business, although in reality the younger girls continue to do JK work through the internet.

There is so much to admire about cultural life in Japan, but what is going on with all these mainstream images of sexualised children? Children are cute. It's totally wrong to look at them and think they're sexy.

'Do you think there is a difference between cute and sexy?' a 50-year-old JK client asked me, while we were discussing his favourite 17-year-old high school girl.

Of course there is a difference! My niece is cute, my dog is cute, the children in my life are cute; grown women like Angelina Jolie are sexy. Established, powerful women who look the part and have got something to say are sexy.

But for the men I spoke to in Japan, that's not how it is. Everywhere I went, from the *chaku ero* shoot to the JK cafés, there were men defending the sexualisation of kids. They didn't understand why it was a huge issue and I found that really confusing. How on earth could you not see that? Why would any grown man think it was OK?

It was so normalised. We were often seeing men in their forties or fifties with successful jobs – grown, smart, 'normal' businessmen – who were keen to look at explicit child pornography.

I kept asking, 'Why do you want to look at this? Why is it appealing to you? Because it isn't appealing to me, so try and explain it to me in layman's terms, so that I can understand what it's about and we're on the same page.'

I never really got the answer to that specifically.

I posed the question everywhere I went, including a manga comic bookstore. Sales of manga comics and graphic novels topped £2 billion in Japan in 2015 – they cover all subjects, topics and genres, including erotica. Some comics contain violent images of child abuse and rape; they are known as 'Lolicon', short for 'Lolita complex', and are banned in the UK. After the UN's child protection envoy called Japan out for not outlawing Lolicon as child pornography, the Japanese government tried to ban it too, but backed down after manga artists and publishers mounted a defence on the grounds of free speech.

I met up with Dan Kanemitsu, an anime expert and translator, in a store that sold X-rated manga comics. I picked up a magazine showing a young girl of maybe four years old biting the pubic hair of an adult man. It was repellent.

'Why do the childlike female characters often look like toddlers, and why do the male images always have to be so dominant, and far older?' I asked him.

'The combination of the dashing male with the innocent female is a very common motif within Japanese manga,' he said.

But the drawing didn't like it was of a dashing male to me. It looked like the depiction of a child abuser.

'Is this child pornography?' I asked Dan.

'That's a very loaded question to ask,' he said, 'because pornography implies it is illegal.'

He was quite good at dodging questions, I'll give him that.

He emphasised that there was a big difference between an actual child being harmed and a depiction of a child being harmed. I couldn't disagree. You could assume that no actual child was harmed to produce the cover of the magazine. It was just lines on paper and it wasn't abusing anyone. But did it encourage men to think that this was acceptable and then play it out in real life?

Dan believed it could be 'a good venting mechanism' for people who had these kinds of fantasies and could curb their urges. Paedophiles, in other words. He also said that people enjoyed it because it was 'absurd', something that couldn't happen.

'But this does happen,' I said, pointing to the picture again.

He soon retreated to safer ground, where he argued that if you ban these comics, you're infringing free speech and you're behaving like the thought police.

While I found the images offensive and would personally ban them, I was still interested in the broader question of why there is such an appetite to see a child-like figure being gang raped by four animations who were supposedly her uncles. What adult man wants to look at that on the way to work? I accept people saying that it's a picture, it's not a real child. I understand that argument, but I wanted to try and understand why a healthy adult would pay for this kind of comic. Why would it be appealing? I buy *Vogue*, *Porter* and *Elle Decoration* because I get joy from looking at the pictures – so what's the appeal of child-sex manga comics, and do they normalise child abuse?

'I know about the laws and I know the free speech argument, but can you just tell me why you'd want to watch children being gang raped?' I asked. 'I understand that you believe it is your right, but why do you want to look at images like that?'

Like everyone else I met on my trip, Dan Kanemitsu was unable to give me a clear or concise answer.

'Are there people in Japan who simply don't realise or recognise that child exploitation is a problem?' I asked Shihoko Fujiwara. She was brilliant; she had just had a baby and was already back at work at her NGO lobbying the government to change laws and attitudes in this area.

'We have a problem in Japan,' she told me. 'We have this history of sexualising children and it's getting worse and worse. What's happening is abuse, and it's not just at 15 or 16. We are seeing three-year-olds, two year-olds being abused.'

'Has it always been this way?' I asked.

'As far as I know, it's been like this for the last 20 years,' she said.

There was a massive gulf between the UK and Japan when it came to child pornography arrests and prosecutions, I discovered. A quick comparison showed that in 2015 and 2016, there were more than 5,000 arrests for possession of child porn in the UK, with 481 found guilty. But in Japan during the same period, only 37 cases were sent to public prosecutors.

I arranged a meeting with Yasuhiru Konishi, the head of the juvenile section at the National Police Agency. Mr Konishi explained that under Japanese law, it's far tougher to bring a prosecution. Before the police can arrest someone for owning an explicit image of a child, they must be sure that the evidence they have will guarantee a conviction. That means they need to identify the child in the image and confirm they are underage. Then the victim has to bring charges.

You've got to ask why they don't make it a bit easier to prosecute these people. Is there an actual, genuine desire to clamp down on this crime?

I started to think the only reason child pornography was made illegal in 2014 was international pressure. It's just my opinion, but I don't think there was any real political will behind it; I don't think it was Japanese authoritative figures saying, 'Actually, we've got to get hold of this.' I think they were shamed into doing it.

Shihoko Fujiwara agreed with me, and she didn't think that banning child pornography would be enough to tackle the problem. To bring about a total shift in attitudes would take a massive media campaign and the complete backing of the Japanese authorities, she said. 'We need to push the society harder to understand that we can't commercialise our own children.'

The film that came out of this trip was called *Young Sex for Sale in Japan* and it was one of the most popular documentaries on iPlayer that year. The commissioner rang me and said, 'It's fantastic, it's exceeded all expectations.'

I don't know why it was so popular – perhaps because everyone is fascinated by Japan and wants to go there. It's just so cool, so impressive and so foreign – and the way it feels so different is what's so exciting about it. I love the country, the food and the fashion. Tokyo is one of my favourite cities in the world. It's amazing, so futuristic and bizarre and beautiful. Expensive is the only thing.

Part of the fascination is that Japan is so different to everywhere else I've been. The Japanese way of life is very sophisticated and luxurious – it isn't difficult like it is for some of the people in the other countries that I've made films in. It's so forward thinking in so many ways – in technology and lifestyle – but there's this one area that's completely weird and backward.

The documentary got a lot of praise, and a lot of its success was down to Joyce. She's a great director and has become a great pal of mine. We've worked together for years, and gone from filming blow jobs together in Magaluf (don't ask; it was one of my earlier films looking at boozed up Brits abroad!) to making some of the films I'm most proud of. She directed the documentaries we made in the Philippines and in Turkey, too.

But there was a huge backlash after the film went out, especially in Japan. People get so outraged when you voice a different opinion to theirs. There was real hatred on Twitter and the anime and manga enthusiasts went ballistic. Some of them were vile, actually. They were saying the most horrific things in tweets and emails.

People were angry that I had the audacity to go over there and ask these questions, as if I was under the illusion that Britain was perfect. 'How dare you even suggest that X-rated anime or manga drawings might play a part in encouraging child abuse?' 'How can an English girl come over and judge us through her views and her cultures?'

I never ever said that, although I understand that they went on the attack to protect their identity. But it wasn't about that. I was in Japan to talk about what was going on in Japan.

I accept that they are entitled to disagree with me on many things, but however much you want to dress it up, child abuse is child abuse. I'm not going to be too frightened to rock the culture boat. Sexualising children is just never acceptable, never OK. For me, it's as straightforward as that. I don't accept it – I'm not having it.

I know I'm in a privileged position and I'm grateful for that every day, but you also have to stick to your guns. You have to be brave enough to stand up and say, 'I don't care whether you think I'm culturally insensitive. This is what I think, based on what I've learned.'

Paedophilia is paedophilia. If you're Japanese, if you're English. Wherever you are, let's call a spade a spade. You've got to have balls and not be frightened about being called a bigot, a racist or somebody who's judgemental. You have to call these things out for what they are and that's what I saw in Japan. I accept that it's not every Japanese person, but it's a nationwide issue that needs resolving.

It's good that the film opened debate and encouraged discussion. As long as people are talking about the subject and thinking about it, I think we've done our job. Things never change overnight, obviously, but you can get people asking questions.

The more I do this job, the more I feel I don't want to tell people what to do or what to think. I want to give them all of this information and then leave it to them to come up with their own conclusions. It's like, That's your shout, but this is what's happening, so take it from there.

10

Amber and Vivian

Murder

Ask most people in the UK what they think of Canada, and they'll bring up Prime Minister Justin Trudeau. He's handsome, he's dashing, he says he's a feminist, he marches at Pride parades and he's generally the poster boy for a forward-thinking and liberal country. Or, if you've had the pleasure of spending time in a city like Vancouver, you'll likely think, Such a comfortable, liberal, settled place, full of beautiful houses and well-off people eating sushi and edamame beans … it's just so lovely!

This is the popular image of Canada, and yet, on the reserves where the indigenous people live, I saw a completely different side of life. Here there was no money, no work and the infrastructure was broken. People's houses were falling down. Some of them didn't even have clean water. It was unthinkable that this was happening in twenty-first-century Canada.

The indigenous, or First Nations, people of Canada are the descendants of the original inhabitants of the land, and include tribes such as the Blackfoot, the Cree, the Iroquois and the Algonquin. They had lived in Canada for thousands of years before the first wave of European explorers arrived in the 1500s.

When the colonists eventually took over their lands, they reserved areas for the 'Indians' to live in. But, 150 years later, it's hard to describe how grim the reserves I saw had become – how dull, cold and isolated they were, stuck in the middle of nowhere. Violence and domestic abuse rates were sky high and a lot of the families were haemorrhaging kids to meth. Everyone was in the same boat. They were all struggling – there was nothing to be joyous or excited about. And no one in authority seemed to care. They were desperately in need of the support and funding that Trudeau promised in his 2015 election campaign.

I travelled to Canada to look at just one piece of this shocking picture – the murder and disappearance of at least 1,200 First Nations women over the last 40 years. I wanted to find out why indigenous women are four times as likely to go missing or be killed than other Canadian women and why so many of the men who murdered them have never been found.

Hundreds of murdered women; hundreds of unsolved cases – and that's just according to police figures. Research from the Native Women's Association of Canada and other organisations put the number of dead and missing women at 4,000. I couldn't believe the figures when I first read about them. It wouldn't sink in. I remember thinking, This can't be right. All these women have been murdered and their killers are still on the loose? What is going on?

I discovered that Canada has a dirty secret that very few of us seem to know about, and Canadians are only just waking up to. And it has had a huge impact on the crimes committed against indigenous women and on the entire community as a whole.

I was in Canada in the winter of 2016/17. One of the first places we filmed was Highway 16 in British Columbia, a massive 700-mile-long road that cuts across the country from east to west, connecting up logging towns and Indian reserves. We filmed in the freezing cold on a desolate stretch of the highway, surrounded by dark, dense woodland, between the cities of Prince George and Prince Rupert. Every ten or fifteen minutes a big Canadian truck would roar past, and that was it. There was nothing else – just a vast, sombre silence.

This section of road is known as the Highway of Tears, because nearly 40 women and girls have died or disappeared there over the years, many of them indigenous and many of them teenagers. Often they were abducted while they were hitchhiking between the logging towns and reserves. Without a local bus service, hitching a ride from a stranger was the only way to get about – to the doctor's, to visit family, to go shopping, on a date or clubbing. So many women never got to where they were heading.

It felt horribly eerie and depressing standing by the side of that deserted road in the pale light of winter. I was shivering with cold even though I had loads of clothes on; I kept thinking about these young girls who would hitch a ride in their hot pants or little skirts and flip flops, because they felt they needed to be done up when they went into town. Knowing the dangers, how did they feel as they got into a truck or car with a lone driver?

We went to the spot by the side of the road where the body of 14-year-old Aielah Auger had been found. She had been mutilated, dismembered and then dumped like a bag of garbage. Aielah's injuries were so horrific that her family couldn't have an open coffin at her funeral.

I couldn't imagine how it must have felt for a young girl to be alone with her killer in this weird, empty landscape, with no one to protect her. Nothing could have been more frightening. It was a really bleak, scary place. I hated to think of the fear and pain she must have gone through.

Aielah Auger's murder was never solved. In fact, no one has been held accountable for any of the murders on the Highway of Tears, according to Raymond Chalco, an ex-cop I spoke to during the making of the programme. I couldn't believe it when he told me that. Forty dead girls and not one person in prison.

Ray said that the police felt they could have solved some of the killings, but in a lot of the cases they weren't given the resources they needed to do a proper investigation. These decisions about allocating resources were made by people higher up in the police department, he said, adding that the authorities didn't care enough about the girls and their communities to spend money looking into what had happened to them. They just weren't important enough, he said. The murders didn't matter.

'Really?' I said. '*Really*?' It was a real struggle to accept what he was alleging.

And then I read about what had happened to Amber Tuccaro, a 20-year-old single mother who went missing in Leduc County on the outskirts of Edmonton in Alberta province, in 2010.

Amber was last seen getting into a vehicle outside a motel, hitching a ride into town. Forty-eight hours later, her worried mum, Vivian, rang the police to report her disappearance. Vivian and Amber were constantly phoning and texting each other so Vivian was really anxious that she hadn't heard from her daughter for so long.

She says the police told her to chill. 'Maybe she's just out partying,' they said, 'and she'll call or she'll come back.'

'I know Amber. I want to report her missing,' Vivian insisted.

But she felt that the police didn't take her seriously – even though four other girls had gone missing or been murdered in the same area.

They didn't try to gather CCTV evidence until it was too late and all the local CCTV film had been recorded over. They didn't answer Vivian's follow-up calls or call her back. It took several days for them to even put Amber on the missing persons list – and two whole years to release a recording of Amber's last phone call from inside the vehicle that picked her up. Yes, you read that correctly. They had a recording of Amber talking to the man who most probably murdered her. She was trying to reach her brother at the Edmonton Remand Centre to ask him to phone the police for her, and the 17-minute call was recorded by the remand centre.

In the recording, you can hear Amber speaking to the unidentified suspect driver, questioning the route he was taking. 'You'd better not be taking me anywhere I don't want to go!' she says, the panic rising in her voice. *You can hear him very clearly telling her to calm down*. It's chilling. You have the strongest sense you're listening to the voice of a killer.

Amber's family believe that if the recording of her last phone call had been put out on TV and radio in the days after she went missing, someone might have recognised the voice of the man speaking to her. It's blindingly obvious – so why did it take the police so long to release it? It just doesn't make sense.

In so many murder cases you have no clue where to start. You have no idea of what happened and no description of the killer. But in this recording they had uniquely precious evidence, where you can actually hear a man's voice. And still you're telling me that you can't find the killer? You can't identify this man when you've got clear audio?

Why were they seemingly so casual in their investigation – and so uncaring in their dealings with Amber's mum and family? Especially as several other women had also disappeared in the vicinity? That fact alone should have set off alarm bells.

I was gobsmacked when I first read Amber's story. I'm not an expert and I don't know what the standard procedure is in dealing with these kind of situations, but it felt like the police investigation was a car crash from start to finish. It's almost as if they didn't want to find Amber or help her. But why?

'To me, they didn't give a shit. They didn't care,' Vivian told me. If I was her, I'd think so, too.

Her pain was so evident. It was devastating. 'If I could have one wish granted it would be to have Amber back,' she kept saying. 'I miss my baby so much – every day, all the time.'

Her grief was still totally raw because she had no answers. She wanted justice for her daughter, and to know what had happened to her. But there was nothing – there was no evidence and no apparent drive to solve the case. I didn't get it. It was the job of the police to try to find out what happened to Amber. They were being paid a decent wage to investigate cases like hers. So why didn't they follow up on the disappearance of a 20-year-old single mum whose family were worried sick about her?

Amber's brother, Paul, put it down to racial prejudice. He was convinced that they didn't properly look into Amber's disappearance because she was a First Nations girl, a member of one of Canada's indigenous communities. He accused the police of institutionalised racism and of stereotyping the native people as lowlife addicts, abusers and prostitutes.

'They think because First Nations girls, you know, they drink, they do drugs, they do all this. So do other nationalities. What makes Indians less important?' he asked bitterly.

'So what if she parties?' said Vivian, breaking into tears. 'So what if she does whatever she wants to do? That doesn't make her less of a human being. She was my baby.'

Raymond Chalco took me to the woods where Amber's body was found, near one of hundreds of side roads off the highway in Leduc County. It was a terrifyingly isolated place – just trees, trees, trees, and no one to hear you scream, for miles and miles into the empty distance. It made my skin crawl.

Ray believed that most murders committed on the highway are carried out by opportunists. No one knows for sure, but maybe a guy picks a girl up and then it goes wrong in some way, or it dawns on him how much power he's got once she's in his car and he's locked the door. When her phone doesn't work because she's got no credit and her mum and sisters don't know where she is, she is at his disposal. Whatever he wants to do, he's going to do. He's totally in charge. He's got all the power.

I agree with Ray that some of the killers are opportunists. I also think some of them set out to kill. To me, these highways linking the reserves with local towns looked like a sexual predator's dream – it's where you would go if you wanted to kill an indigenous woman, isn't it? A killer operating on these roads can pretty much assume he won't be caught, because the murder of an indigenous woman won't be followed up in the way that it would be if she was a white woman. Statistically, he will get away with it. None of the Highway of Tears murderers are in prison. We still have no idea who killed Amber in Leduc County.

So what do we know about the men who are committing these crimes, apart from the fact that they are mentally unwell? It's hard to know anything. All you can do is guess. Maybe the man who killed Amber was somebody who had a fetish for indigenous women, or he decided he could get away with it because she was indigenous. Or maybe Amber just happened to come along and he realised how easy it would be to kill her. There are a lot of indigenous women out there living chaotic lives, so it's inevitable that predators will come across them.

As I looked further into Amber Tuccaro's murder and the holes in the police investigation, the evidence suggested that assumptions had been made about Amber because she was from the reserve and of aboriginal descent. Her brother seemed to be right about the stereotyping of First Nations girls. The prejudice against them is widespread from the ground up – and it's partly a consequence of the poverty and deprivation that has pushed so many of them onto the streets.

I travelled to Edmonton, a city with a population of around a million, where up to 90 per cent of women working on the streets in the sex trade were of indigenous descent. A lot of them were homeless and addicted to drugs. They were horribly vulnerable. A shocking number had gone missing or been murdered over the years.

I went out on the streets at night with Kari Thomason, a social worker who has been providing support and rehabilitation to Edmonton's highest risk sex workers for 20 years. Kari was really amazing. She worked so hard trying to help these girls and keep them safe.

In an area of the city notorious for sex workers' murders, she introduced me to Tee, a 30-year-old prostitute who was three months pregnant. I asked Tee what it was like out working on the street.

'It's scary, lonely and horrible,' she said bluntly, and tears began to roll down her face.

Kari told me that Tee had first been pimped out as a child – at the age of ten – by her own mother. 'Just knowing the shit that kid's going through, you know, it sucks,' Kari said, herself close to tears. 'Her mum was an active addict, and you need that fix, and sometimes you do some God-awful evil things, and sometimes you sacrifice your child for the dope,' she explained.

I went back to my room that night feeling tired and deflated. Tee's existence was so depressing, and so predictable once you knew what had happened to her as a child. I felt there was no hope for her because, with that as your starting point in life, how on earth can you expect to flourish or succeed – or even have a fair chance or a good go at things? I wanted to hate her mother, but I didn't know what she had been through to make her do such a thing to her daughter. It made me feel so grateful for the childhood I'd had. Compared to other people in England I didn't have a privileged upbringing, but compared to the girls I met on the Edmonton streets, I won the lottery.

Tee said, 'I'm cold. I'm cold,' and some outreach workers gave her a pair of gloves. It was so kind of them to be out there helping on the freezing cold streets at night, but in the grand scheme of things I couldn't help thinking, What difference is a pair of gloves going to make? She needs intervention. She needed help when she was a kid and her addicted, prostitute mum exploited her to pay for her habit. It was shocking. I mean, it was one thing reading the statistics, but meeting the girls out there on those bleak streets at night really brought home the hopelessness of the situation.

Kari explained that a lot of indigenous girls are groomed at a young age, often by members of their own community. It's usually men, who pay attention to the girls they target and treat them like a boyfriend would, making them feel special before taking them to the city and pimping them. Since the girls have grown up surrounded by abuse and addiction, they often don't know what a healthy relationship looks like. So they fall for it, hook, line and sinker.

Among the 900 women on Kari's database was Shelley, a street sex worker who told me that she had been abused between the ages of 8 and 13. She started working as a prostitute at 18.

'I was put on the street by my boyfriend at the time,' she said. 'He stuck a needle in my arm and that's how it went. So it was a snowball effect, and if I didn't get abused by him, I got abused by the drug dealers. If I didn't get abused by the drug dealers, I was getting abused by my family.'

I had to ask Kari what was going wrong in these communities for this to be happening. Why were there so many social problems on the reserves? Obviously they were horribly affected by poverty and deprivation, but did it go further and deeper than that?

Actually, it was my assistant producer who gave me my first hint about the underlying cause of a lot of the misery and social breakdown. We were on a boat in Vancouver talking through the programme's contributors when she said, 'You know, so many of these people were thrown into residential schools.'

'What's a residential school?' I asked.

When she explained, my jaw hit the deck. I remember thinking, You have got to be kidding!

I already knew that European colonisation had devastated the native population, pushing the indigenous people onto the fringes of society and into state-funded reserves. I knew that the communities on these reserves suffered from chronic unemployment, substance abuse and domestic violence. But I had *no idea at all* that, for a hundred years, indigenous children were ripped from their families by the government and placed in church-run boarding houses to learn white Christian values. I don't think the majority of white Canadians knew about it, either. These boarding houses were the residential schools my AP had been talking about – and the last of them wasn't closed until 1996.

At a remote reserve on the outskirts of Fort Chipewyan in northern Alberta, Steve Courtoreille, the reserve's chief, showed me round the residential school that he had been forced to attend for ten years, from the age of five. Steve seemed amazingly calm as he described the relentless barrage of physical, mental, spiritual and emotional abuse he had suffered. Somehow he had managed to digest what had gone on; he seemed to have reached an incredible level of acceptance. I admired him for it, because it's very easy to hold onto hate and anger and angst, and to let them win. But he had transcended his experience and was now desperate to continue with the rest of his life.

Steve told me that the purpose of the residential schools was to 'take the Indian out' of the First Nations people, strip them of their culture and 'turn them into human beings'. He recalled being told on a daily basis that he was a savage and 'good for nothing'. He experienced physical beatings and, later on, sexual abuse – and there was no one to turn to for help. To think that this went on in a state-funded, church-run school – and that 150,000 children endured the cruelty of the system – is totally horrific. That it was still going on in my lifetime is mind blowing.

There was one story that really stuck with me. In fact, out of all the documentaries I've worked on, it's probably the one I think about the most. Steve said that the kids weren't allowed to go within a certain distance of the school fence inside the compound, because they were banned from communicating with family members who walked anywhere near the school. They couldn't wave to their mums and dads through the fence; they couldn't say, 'I love you', or express any affection at all. Nothing was allowed to interfere with killing the savage. They weren't really allowed to have mums and dads, or families at all.

It's one of the saddest things I've ever heard.

'The biggest damage that was done was they destroyed the families and the extended family concept,' Steve explained.

Clearly the consequences are still being felt throughout the indigenous communities, and the shockwaves will probably reverberate for generations. It is common knowledge, after all, that sometimes the abused becomes the abuser. It's learned behaviour.

'There's a lot of violence, a lot of family break-ups,' Steve agreed.

For many of the women, the only way to escape abuse and to keep their children safe has been to leave and go to the city. 'And where else would they end up?' he asked. 'In the streets of Edmonton, Fort McMurray, Calgary, Toronto, wherever.'

In 2008, the Truth and Reconciliation Committee of Canada was established to respond to the abuse inflicted on indigenous people by the residential school system and to explore its legacy. It was set up after ex-students of the schools brought the largest class action in Canada's history against the federal government and four national churches. Part of the out-of-court settlement was to establish the Committee, which awarded on average $20,000 to former students. That's about £12,000 per lost childhood.

During the next seven years, the Committee took testimony from thousands of people who had been subjected to the cruelty of the system, and made a series of recommendations as to how the legacy of problems could be redressed. But when I spoke to people on the reserves and elsewhere about whether they thought it had achieved anything, my overriding impression was that they would have preferred to see the multi-million budget spent in a more productive way.

I mean, I'm not an expert when it comes to transport and safety, but don't tell me that you couldn't put on a couple of buses when you know that one of the main reasons indigenous girls are hitchhiking is because there's no other means of getting to the shops or the doctor's. They might be going to pick up drugs, yes. They might be going to sell themselves. But laying on a couple of buses to ensure their safety is surely worth the expense.

For a lot of the women I spoke to, the report merely confirmed what they already knew, because they were living it. It was their reality. 'We want the millions to be spent on actual change,' they were saying. 'Give us some buses. Give us clean drinking water. Give us homes that don't fall down.'

I would have loved the chance to speak to Justin Trudeau about it. We went to his office and tried to engage him, but for some reason or another it didn't happen.

I would have said, 'You need to invest in these reserves and you need to make sure that these women are as valued and protected as white Canadians are. Don't tell me that if these girls were white girls with blonde hair and blue eyes then this wouldn't be dealt with differently, because I'd find it really hard to believe. It's just my personal opinion, of course – but I would like to know what you think, too.'

In August 2016, Trudeau's government launched a $40 million inquiry into the murders and disappearances of 1,200 aboriginal women. This was the figure mentioned in a 2014 report by the Royal Canadian Mounted Police (RCMP), but since then at least two government ministers have put it at nearer 4,000. Trudeau promised a 'total renewal' of Canada's relationship with its indigenous population. It was an ambitious project and expectations were high, but within a year the inquiry was mired in problems.

The victims' families started protesting that they were being left out of the process. One of the five commissioners heading the inquiry resigned because she felt colonial bias was obstructing the process and many First Nations people felt that the murders and disappearances of these women were being looked at through racist, colonialist eyes. So no one was getting anywhere – and a lot of the victims' families felt traumatised all over again.

Finally, 150 indigenous leaders, activists and family members wrote to Trudeau asking him to halt the inquiry, criticising it for being disorganised and lacking in transparency.

'The time has come to restart this top-down inquiry and to rebuild it from the ground up,' they wrote.

No inquiry will bring Amber Tuccaro back. But it would be worth any amount of money to prevent further murders like hers – and to bring about change in the culture of the police departments investigating them, if necessary. I spoke to several people who blamed the lack of investigation into Amber's death on racism. One of them was Lorimer Shenher, who was a detective for the Vancouver Police Department for two decades. Lorimer had been one of the lead investigators in Canada's biggest serial killer case: Robert Pickton, a pig farmer who was eventually charged with the murders of 27 women, most of them indigenous, and is thought to have killed as many as 49 women.

Lorimer said that the police missed an unbelievable number of leads that could have led them to Pickton earlier, saving 14 or 15 women's lives. In his opinion it was a clear case of institutional racism.

'This file just kept getting put on the corner of people's desks, and I kept checking in with them week after week, month after month, only to find out that they really weren't doing anything,' he told me.

'I think that a lot of the families and the women involved in our investigation had very frustrating interactions with our office staff over the years. I heard my own secretary saying, "Speak Canadian. This is Canada. Speak English." Talking to them like they're deaf and stupid. And you would get told you're a bad parent. It was your fault that they were on the street in the first place. That you're an alcoholic or drug user yourself. These were things that I heard being said to the family members.'

By people they were supposed to be able to rely on.

Lorimer said that the way Amber's disappearance was investigated was typical of the police response in thousands of similar cases, all over the country. It was incredible to hear a member of the police confirming what I had been told time and again by indigenous people.

It is almost as if some authoritative figures are willing to write these girls off because they live a high-risk lifestyle. And some of them do, let's be honest – no one is making out that they live perfect lives. Some of them live really chaotic lives. But Vivian deserves to know who killed her daughter, surely?

The RCMP wouldn't talk to me about the specifics of Amber's case, but they agreed for me to meet Superintendent Gary Steinke, a senior officer from their Alberta provincial headquarters. He said he hadn't come across any racist individuals in the force, although he agreed that there probably were racists in the police, 'like there are in every other walk of life'.

I said that I had spoken about Amber Tuccaro's case to two non-family members who felt that the RCMP were, at best, incompetent and, at worst, blatantly racist.

'We're not incompetent,' he said. 'We do want to solve these cases, regardless of gender or race.'

It was good to hear him say so, but I put it to him that many of the victims' families believed that if their daughter had been Caucasian and blue-eyed with blonde hair, there would have been more of a sense of urgency in the investigation.

'The 72 hours after the individual's gone missing is crucial, and I think that's why Amber Tuccaro's mother feels so let down, because there was no sense of urgency,' I explained.

'I think mistakes were made in that particular case, and she knows that,' he conceded. 'And we've apologised for that.'

'They feel totally let down. They have no faith in you whatsoever,' I said.

'As of today, and in years past, the RCMP have learned lessons, as every police organisation has,' he assured me. 'Some of these cases are very, very difficult to solve. All I can say is that every single case, and the one you've mentioned here, is still under investigation.'

Superintendent Steinke seemed genuine about his commitment to finding out what happened to the women we were discussing. He appeared to agree that it shouldn't have mattered if Amber was brown, if she was white, where she came from, if she did drugs or didn't do drugs, if she was a prostitute or wasn't a prostitute. She was someone's daughter. She was a woman. And she was a mother.

So many of the murdered women have left behind young children. This alone should be enough to make the government do more. Amber Tuccaro's son, Jacob, was seven when I met him. Vivian was bringing him up.

It broke Vivian's heart every time Jacob asked, 'Where's Mama? Where is she?'

He was such a little sweetheart, that lad. Vivian told me that when he started school on the reserve, all the kids teased him that he didn't have a mum. And then, when we turned up with the cameras, they taunted him by saying, 'The only reason they're filming here is because your mum's dead.'

They were only being kids – and they obviously felt a bit envious that the spotlight was on him – but I felt so sorry for him. Like so many motherless children in indigenous communities across Canada, he needed his mum. Her death left a gaping hole in his life, in her family and in the whole community. And her killer was still out there.

The unsolved murders of so many indigenous women in Canada is a national disgrace. And although police attitudes may be changing, the problems for indigenous girls remain the same. Is there any way of changing things? Clearly the infrastructure on the reserves needs massive improvement and there should be more investment in jobs and education for indigenous communities. The government needs to try and make sure that the indigenous people have as many opportunities as all the other Canadians.

I think it's that straightforward, but it doesn't make it simple. I just hope something is done soon to improve the conditions of the people living on the reserves so that indigenous women don't feel they have to go on risking life and limb on Canada's highways and city streets.

11

The Yazidi Women

War

In July 2016, I had a call from Gian, my commissioner at BBC3.

'There's this idea that I think would potentially be fascinating, and I think it could be a really good gig for you to do,' he said. 'But it involves going to northern Iraq and you'd be on the frontline where the Kurds and Iraqis are fighting Isis, although that would only be a very small section of the film,' he added. 'How would you feel about that?'

Um …

He explained that the film would be focusing on a group of Yazidi women and what they'd been through. It would be quite immersive and I would live alongside them.

'OK, cool, let me have a think and read up about them,' I said.

I didn't know anything about the Yazidi women. I'd never even heard of them. I didn't know what their situation was at all.

'There's no rush, no pressure,' he said. 'It's your shout. Whatever you're thinking, just let me know.'

I started researching the Yazidi population in the Sinjar – or Shingal – district of northern Iraq, which is about 80 miles away from Mosul. A few articles popped up, mostly from 2014. They were horrifying. I discovered that these Kurdish-speaking people are one of Iraq's oldest minority communities and mostly live in the Nineveh Province. They have their own distinct culture and traditions and practise their own religion. In 2014, the Islamic fundamentalist militant group, Isis, attacked the area in and around the city of Sinjar as part of its drive to establish a worldwide 'caliphate', tearing down villages and massacring thousands of Yazidi people. They killed all the men first – in front of the women. Then they murdered a lot of the disabled women because they were of no use to them. Finally, they kidnapped more than 5,000 girls and women to use as sex slaves.

In 2016, when Gian rang me, around 3,000 women were still in captivity behind the Isis lines, where they were being beaten, raped, tortured and abused every day.

This is unbelievable! I thought. How is it I don't know about this?

I hadn't heard of a story like it. We were all familiar with the Boko Haram kidnapping of hundreds of Nigerian schoolgirls in 2014 because it was all across the news – and rightly so. I remembered Michelle Obama and other well-known people holding up signs saying, 'Bring Back Our Girls'. But there was no global outrage over the thousands of Yazidi girls kidnapped by Isis. There was hardly any media coverage at all – just a few stray reports. Why? I couldn't understand it.

The Yazidis have been persecuted throughout history. Their religion is thought to be pre-Islamic and it's very spiritual, from what I understand; they worship an ancient god and pray facing the sun. But Isis sympathisers believe that they are devil worshippers, and Isis fighters specifically targeted Sinjar because to them the Yazidis were the lowest of the low, and so they felt they had the right to kill the men and rape the women. It really was that black and white for them: you are followers of Satan. You aren't human. You don't deserve to be treated as such. No one was off limits. Babies and children were there to be abused too – they took or destroyed anything they wanted.

I read some horrific accounts by Yazidi women who had been kidnapped by Isis. Many of them had been raped consistently – not once or twice, but numerous times a day. The rapes were particularly violent and the men exceptionally cruel and abusive because they thought the Yazidi women were totally disposable, there to be shagged, abused and dictated to.

Often the fighters' wives would help the men abuse them. There was no sense of sisterhood there whatsoever – you couldn't rely on the women already on the scene because they hated you as much as their husbands did. In fact, there was a bit of jealousy there sometimes. 'My man's raping you so much of the time that he's actually having sex with you more than he is with me.'

So they faced hostility on all sides.

They'd had to watch and wait for a chance to get away. One girl found some money in a drawer; another found an unattended phone. Another said that her 'owner' had left the back door open and she was able to slip outside. It was so brave of her. She ran and ran and ran; eventually she found a taxi driver and pleaded with him to take her to safety.

There were stories about good Samaritans who helped the girls out by driving them away or letting them use their phones to call a relative. There were smugglers who helped as well, but any escape required careful planning. I don't know if I would have the courage even to try, because I'd be thinking, There's no way I'm going to get away with this. But if you'd rather be dead than alive, given your circumstances, what have you got to lose? That's how a lot of them said they felt. They were at their wits' end.

For the documentary, I was going to spend just over two weeks living with a truly amazing group of Yazidi women who were fighting back. They were determined to avenge the genocide and mass kidnapping of 2014. Their aim was to rescue the women still in captivity – their sisters, cousins, mothers, aunts and nieces. And so these women had joined the Peshmerga Army, the military forces of the Kurdish Region of Iraq. Now they were armed and in training for battle on the Isis frontline.

Most of them had been kidnapped by Isis and had somehow escaped. I found it incredible that instead of running away from the horrors they had seen and experienced, they were now turning back to face their abusers. It seemed unbelievable. They were beyond brave.

Had these girls always known war and struggle? Actually, no. They had been living in very calm, very simple conditions for their entire lives. Some of them were housewives and mothers; many of them went to work every day on the high street: at the fruit stall, sewing clothes or cutting hair. They were typical, relatable women who had never thought of entering the military. But as soon as Isis came, their whole reality was completely flipped on its head and they were forced to fight back.

I went back to Gian and said, 'Yeah, I definitely want to do this. But I need to meet the crew because I want to go with a really straight, together team.'

Some of the directors you work with are super clever and bright, but they're also very off the cuff and maverick. I thought, I'm not going to Iraq with any loose cannons!

I went to meet Helen and Almudena, who are really good pals now. I'd already worked with the director, Almudena – she was my sister, *mi hermana* – and so I knew how brilliant she was. But it was my first time meeting Helen, the assistant producer. She was young, bright, and seemed really capable and passionate about the project.

We got out a map and worked out the logistics. There were loads of zones coloured in red, and red meant high risk. Basically, the entire trip was going to be high risk. It was proper, serious, hardcore journalism. The only other foreigners out there were war reporters.

At this point I had committed to going, but I'd said to my agent, 'Don't take any money. Let's not sign anything. Because if I want to pull out, I don't want them to have me by the balls. If I don't want to do it, I'm not doing it.'

It was the first time I'd done anything so dangerous, the first time I'd been genuinely apprehensive. So even though I really wanted to work on the project, I was still thinking, I might not do this.

I'd been to Mexico, where there was crazy violence and mayhem seemingly on every street corner – but some areas of Mexico are scary and other areas aren't. If you play it right in Mexico, you can very quickly get to the more peaceful parts of the country. But there's nowhere in Iraq you can feel totally safe.

My mind went back and forth, back and forth. As I read more detailed accounts of what the Yazidi girls had gone through, I felt that if I didn't go I would be really pissed off at myself and feel like a fraud. Because you can't say you stand alongside girls and be up for using your voice because you recognise that so many girls around the world don't have a voice and then turn down a unique opportunity to show potentially millions of people what's going on. The girls wanted to tell their story, however painful. I felt I had a responsibility to help them get the word out.

But I was also thinking, I really don't want to die! If something does go wrong, my mother is going to be in bits, and my little sister too. It would shatter my family. And I'm only late twenties; I've got so much I want to achieve.

I wasn't scared of being shot or stabbed; I was scared of being kidnapped and of not being able to get away. I kept playing through a scene in my head of somebody ringing my mother to say, 'They've got Stacey.' She would be totally devastated.

But then I'd think, Stacey, you believe in this and you can't not do things because you're frightened. You've got to be the woman that stands up and has something to say.

It was a genuine roundabout, up and down, back and forth in my mind. I tried to get some comfort from the thought that the channel wouldn't have commissioned it if they genuinely thought we could die. I would be with Iraqi officials who were in charge of the safer areas. You have to trust people, I thought. You have to trust that they're able to keep you safe.

I told myself that I'd committed and I was going. But the doubts kept creeping back. I was haunted by the idea that we would be so close to Isis-controlled Mosul, even though the battle had begun to liberate the city and hopefully it wouldn't take too long.

The night before we went, I was packing and I suddenly thought, What am I doing? Why on earth am I voluntarily walking in the direction that everybody else is running from? Am I biting off more than I can chew? Is this a bit too grown up and too big for me? I burst into tears.

'I'm so scared,' I said to Sam. 'I really want to do it, but I don't want to go!'

He gave me a hug. 'Stacey, if you don't do it, honest to God, you will just kick yourself for years to come,' he said. 'I honestly think you should go.'

I knew he was right, but I was also thinking, Why are you so keen for me to go to Iraq? What kind of a boyfriend are you?!

I think he underestimated how nervous I was. In his mind, they wouldn't send me if I was going to die, so he'd convinced himself it was fine.

I woke up the next morning, made my way to Turkey, got a flight to Erbil, the capital of the Kurdistan Region in northern Iraq, and then from Erbil I travelled down to Sinjar and the frontline. I told my mum I was going to Turkey for a couple of weeks. There would have been no use telling her the truth because she would have been out of her mind with worry the whole time. Sometimes when you hear about these places you can imagine that perhaps it's worse than it actually is, and I thought that her anxiety would make me feel more anxious. So even if she would have liked to know, there was just no way I was going to tell her.

It sounds cheesy, but I felt empowered as soon as I got to the camp, where a group of Yazidi girls were being trained to be soldiers by members of the Peshmerga Kurdish Army. All of a sudden there were all these strong women coming up to me, saying hello and slapping my shoulder, practically knocking me to the ground because they didn't realise their own strength. They were very tactile, instantly welcoming; there was no having to break the ice. It was a relief to be around them and they were grateful in turn that we were there telling their story, because it hadn't been reported in the way that it should have been.

These were the strongest women I've ever met. Many of them had escaped after being held captive by Isis for weeks, months or years. If you can survive being an Isis hostage and you have the audacity, strength and belief to escape – well, I don't know anyone who is stronger than that.

One girl told me that when Isis came to Sinjar and killed the men and disabled women, they divided the rest of the women up. The beautiful ones were stood here and the unremarkable ones there. Then the Isis fighters gave them razors and soap and told them to go and wash and fix themselves up, ready for sex. One girl said, 'I'll go first.' She took her soap and the razor, went to the bathroom, closed the door and slit her wrists. The others didn't know what she'd done until blood started pouring under the door.

She obviously knew what was coming.

It was like a horror film. Young girls were raped, some as young at eight. Babies were killed in front of their mums. During religious celebrations, the fighters would swap girls or give each other girls.

I've come face to face with evil – I've met a lot of evil individuals over the years. I've spent time with drug dealers and narco bosses and people working for cartels who have done horrific things. But in my mind Isis were in a league of their own. It was hard to get my head around that level of cruelty and inhumanity. It was just so dark and so brutal. And it didn't just last a week. For the thousands of girls who were still prisoners of Isis, it had been years of abuse.

You just don't know what you would do in that situation. Would you try to save yourself the horrors and not give them the satisfaction of being able to touch you? Would you kill yourself? Would you slit your wrists, or continue to fight through in the hope that one day you'd be able to escape?

Xate Shingali was one of the older girls in charge at the camp when I arrived. Xate had started the battalion by recruiting girls from the refugee camps after Isis took control. She was lovely – and quite surprising: before she joined the military, she was a massive pop star. She had vowed not to sing again until all the Yazidi women and girls still in captivity had been returned to their communities.

The Yazidi community were totally behind her and the other girls who had decided to join Peshmerga and train to be soldiers, and I heard quite a few people express regret that the women hadn't had any military training before the Isis attack. 'If the women had known how to use guns, things might have been different,' a Peshmerga soldier told me.

When I got to the camp, Xate took my bag and pushed me into a room where the unit were getting ready to go to sleep. 'Off you go!'

The other girls were really inquisitive about me. 'Who is she?' They gathered round to play with my hair and count my mosquito bites. It was very odd for them to have me there, so they were almost picking at me, like a gorilla with a little baby.

My first night, I slept on the top bunk of a bunk bed. The light was on all night; it was so, so hot; I heard rogue gunfire shots every now and then. Still, I felt safer and calmer than expected. I was thinking, If anybody does come for us, so many of these girls have got guns that although I might get shot accidentally, at least they will be able to defend us. But I didn't sleep for more than an hour at a time, and it was very light sleep. You're in and out of consciousness, because you're constantly waiting for something to happen.

The next day we moved to a training camp in Snuny, in a building that had once been a high school. Isis had taken it over and made it their headquarters for a few months; the Yazidis had since taken it back. It was weird being based somewhere Isis had spent so long – it was their fighters' base and there were Isis flags all over the walls, painted over, but still visible. You couldn't help imagining. You'd be sat there eating cucumber, which is all we had for dinner because the food supplies were low, thinking, What went on in here? What happened?

We slept on the roof of the building, which was a blessing and a curse. The roof was actually more comfortable than the bunk bed because it was cooler, darker and I didn't have a light shining in my face. But we were closer to the frontline than before, so it was more frightening. And there were mice everywhere.

'Do you like mice? Are you scared of them?' the girls asked.

'I absolutely hate mice!' I said.

But there's no avoiding them when you're sleeping on the floor.

Every night, two girls patrolled the roof with guns, so if anyone or thing was coming towards us, they'd be able to wake us all up. It was scary, but we'd sometimes have a giggle up there. The girls were very soft, very kind and very young in so many ways. The war hadn't hardened them – and I found that inspirational.

It was such an odd situation. I was in a high school littered with reminders of the horror of Isis, I was sleeping on the roof and there were mice everywhere. I hadn't washed properly in a week and a half so I felt itchy. I brushed my teeth every couple of days because there was only one tube of toothpaste between everyone. We ate cucumber and tomato with salt, morning, noon and night. We only had a few teabags, so we could only have one cup of tea a day. And we were getting ready to go over the mountain to the Isis frontline.

There were fleeting moments of light relief. One day we all had headaches, I was starving all the time and Almudena had this little lunchbox full of baby foods from Boots that she'd been saving – mango purée, that sort of thing. I was delighted with this. I remember eating a sachet of baby food and thinking, This is so good! I was really quite slight by the end of the trip. The cameras are heavy, it's hot and you're nervous; the weight falls off you.

Another day, after a wash, we got out our fancy creams – and suddenly our world came into view again. 'Do you want to try this cream? I got it from Space NK.'

'Ooh, that feels really nice!'

'Hey, I like your scarf.'

'Thanks, it's a 100 per cent raw silk.'

But most of the time, we lived in a state of high tension. It was tiring to be scared all the time – I'd underestimated how exhausting it would be. It wasn't like I was sliding down the walls in fear because I couldn't handle the anxiety, but every single minute of the day there was a nagging sensation in the back of my mind that things could kick off at any moment. Even when I was lying down, in and out of sleep, one ear was waiting for a gun to go off.

There was no part of me that enjoyed it. I kept thinking, What am I doing here? Why did I let this happen? You sort of have an argument with yourself in your own mind. You think, Well, you voluntarily got on the plane; no one forced you to come here. Just get on with it.

Almudena and Helen seemed to be a lot calmer than I was, although maybe I was just a bit more verbal about it than they were. Almudena had done quite a few tough gigs and worked in South America, so she was used to doing things that were fairly scary. But it was the Helen the assistant producer's first gig! This is one of the reasons I respect Helen so much and she has a really special place in my heart. She's a fierce young woman who is desperate to make documentaries that she believes are going to provoke change. She's a star.

I didn't see any fear among the Yazidi girls. They were women who couldn't be stopped. They were warriors. I had never met women like them. I think they had probably been very, very frightened when they were captured, but now I felt only strength and determination in them.

It was common knowledge what the vast majority of them had been through – but there was a lot of shame and embarrassment from some of them when it came to talking about it. Instead they'd say, 'This happened to my friend,' or 'my pal's cousin'. It was always one step removed. They had been through all of this and had come back fighting, but shame and honour were still such huge issues for them. It's something that exists in loads of cultures, of course, but I was sad to hear that a few of the girls who escaped weren't welcomed back by their families. Usually it was the dad who couldn't come to terms with the abuse his daughter had suffered. I would hope and pray that they were the minority and that the victims' families recognised at some point that it was never a choice for their girls. After all they had been through, it's heartbreaking to think of them being rejected by the people they needed most.

It's a difficult one to get right: you're there to tell the story, make a documentary and show an accurate picture of what went on and what these girls have been through, but you also don't want to disrespect them or make them feel embarrassed. So you've got to push to try and get the truth – but you can't question it if they're saying to you, point blank, 'Oh no, I was never raped, but my friend was.'

You've got to allow them to tell you what they've got to tell you – but it was hard, because we had the exec on the massive field phone saying, 'We need a story!'

You forget, because you're there and you're so immersed, that there are people in London who want a decent documentary brought back.

One girl started to open up in the schoolroom but then she started sobbing hysterically and ran out of the room. It was obvious what the reality was and I couldn't ask her any more. These girls have already been through enough. Some of them have lost all of their family and loved ones. You don't want them to feel like you're not on their side.

The girls were my number one priority. You need to be able to look at yourself in a mirror at the end of a day's filming and feel totally happy with how you've treated those around you. You have to ask yourself, If I were in their situation, would I feel like I've been treated with respect?

But I also can't bring back a load of rushes showing me and the girls dancing and singing and not talking about anything uncomfortable or serious.

I visited one of the refugee camps with 17-year-old Inas, a fearless soldier who had faced off an Isis fighter with a sword to save her dad from being killed. Inas's sister had been brutally killed when Isis attacked and Inas was determined to avenge her death. Her father seemed very forward thinking. He was proud of his daughter for joining the army.

Inas had been captured, but didn't say for how long or what happened to her. Instead she introduced me to her cousin, one of the few Yazidi girls who felt she could speak openly about the horrific things that had gone on, although she didn't want to reveal her identity on film. Bravely she told me that she had been captured, raped and beaten over and over again for more than a year.

Although she had escaped, she was continually reliving what she had been through, she said. All the while she was awake – while she was eating and talking, even when she was laughing – there were horrific images of Isis brutality before her eyes. The post-traumatic stress never left her. Every day was an uphill struggle.

I've since read accounts by therapists who have provided counselling at the refugee camps to girls like Inas's cousin. They say: 'We have never dealt with women so traumatised. We have never heard stories like the ones coming out of these girls' mouths. It's unprecedented. We've got nothing to compare it to. In all our careers we have never seen anything as bad.'

I can hardly imagine it, especially as rape is one of my biggest fears. Being stabbed, being shot – if it happens, it happens. But rape is so intrusive. And that's why I have such respect and admiration – and love, really – for women who have been raped and have survived to come through it the other end and continue. They are so bloody impressive, so bloody brave.

There was an atmosphere of complete determination as we journeyed in trucks towards the frontline. There was a real sense of strength and optimism among the girls.

'I am happy,' one of them told me. 'I feel like I am going to a wedding.'

'I hope we're not. I'd have to put a dress on,' I said.

'What I am wearing is my most beautiful wedding dress,' she said, glancing down at her uniform and then looking out into the distance and the mountains. It was a very poignant remark; my heart went out to her.

'Where was your country when we were attacked?' another girl asked me. 'Why didn't you come and help us?'

I didn't have an answer. I just explained that I was the wrong person to be asking because I wasn't anywhere near important enough to be involved in those decisions.

I was terrified of going over the mountain and I hated being on the frontline when we got there. There was constant gunfire and mortar shelling, and we were so close to the fighting. In the far distance, I could see the Isis base.

I knew that if I got out alive I would never, ever want to go back. I remember thinking, Get everything you need for this film now, because there's no way on earth that you can put yourself through this again.

It sounds ridiculous, because I was there for just over two weeks and the girls had been there for years. That's why I was so in awe of them. I've met so many impressive women but those girls take it to a whole other level. They were so bold and fierce, driven by the thought that so many of their relatives were still held captive in Mosul and Raqqa.

These were very accessible, relatable women who loved dancing, loved a giggle and couldn't be less like militant warriors. Then as soon as they put their uniform on and went to the frontline, it was like, 'No, we're not taking it! We've had enough.'

I think it must get to that point where you've been raped hundreds of times; you've been sold; you've been given as a gift for Eid from one fighter to another. You've seen your best mate die; you've seen the girl next to you slit her wrists when she was meant to go to the toilet to clean herself up. You've seen Isis fighters raping a nine-year-old. When you have lived through hell and you come out the other side, what is there to be scared of? There's nothing else to fear because every horrendous thing you could imagine has already happened.

What Isis have done, really, is empower these women. They have given these girls a platform. It's the exact opposite of what Isis wished, because these girls are now a force to be reckoned with. They are so resilient.

I was relieved to leave the frontline. I got off the plane at Istanbul, exhaled and thought, It's over. I'm not going to get taken. I'm safe.

It sounds really right on, but I will never take for granted what a privilege it is to live in a society where we're not constantly frightened all of the time.

I rang my mother from the airport. 'Mum, I'm ringing so you don't hear it from anybody else,' I said. 'I've not been in Turkey. I've been in Iraq. But I'm back now, so you don't need to worry.'

She had the hump and wouldn't speak to me for three days.

It took much longer than we expected for Mosul to fall. I was out there in September and they thought it would be over in a matter of weeks – certainly a few months maximum. It took a lot longer because, as we predicted at the end of the documentary, Isis started using prisoners as human shields and it turned into carnage. It was total chaos.

So, although I believe that all the girls in the unit are still alive at this point, there's no way of truly knowing. I hope they are. They are the most inspirational women I have ever met or am likely to meet.

All power to them.

12

Shereen

Survival

I was never, ever, *ever* going back to northern Iraq.

When I stepped onto that plane to Istanbul, after two weeks with the Yazidi girls on the frontline, I definitely said, 'I'm never coming back!' But … it seemed that everyone who watched *Girls, Guns and Isis* was touched by the Yazidis and in awe of these girls. So many people hadn't known about them – in the same way that I hadn't – so there was always talk of the Yazidis everywhere I went: 'How are they doing, those amazing, brave girls?'

Assistant producer Helen and the production team were keen to follow up with a second documentary, so we began working on ideas. We'd kept in touch with a couple of the girls and it felt like a no-brainer to find out how they were doing, a year on. I hadn't forgotten how frightened I'd been in Iraq, but I kept thinking how awesome it would be for the Yazidi girls to have another burst of publicity.

As usual, I went back and forth in my mind.

Gian, our commissioner at BBC3, wasn't sure for a long time. There were ideas he liked in the treatment, which is a plan of the proposed programme – but others he didn't. Helen and I worked hard to get it right, even though in my heart I wasn't planning to go back to Iraq – I honestly wasn't. Then again, I must have been, subconsciously.

The breakthrough came when we secured access to a prison that was holding Isis fighters. The prison officials said, 'You can come in. You can speak to a member of Isis. You can bring a Yazidi girl to him and she can have her say.'

It was unbelievable access.

Finally, it got to a point when Gian was happy with the treatment. 'OK, cool, you can go,' he said.

As soon as he said it, I thought, Oh no!

Things moved really quickly after that. I managed to convince myself that this time was going to be easier. And it was on paper, because when I made the first documentary, Isis were still in Iraq, but now we were going back three months after Isis had been taken out of Mosul. Everything was calming down and there wasn't going to be as much of an Isis presence. Actually, I thought to myself, it should be pretty straightforward. The director we're going with has done tons of filming in Iraq. I think we'll be fine.

Before I went, I needed to redo my hostile environment training course. I'd originally done it in my early twenties, in preparation for some of the hairier documentaries I worked on, but now it was out of date. It's a five-day course where a team of ex-soldiers put you through all of the scenarios that could present themselves in dangerous places. You go to a freezing cold field and they pretend to shoot at you. You learn to give emergency first aid to car-crash victims and bomb victims whose limbs have been blown off. On the last day, they fake-kidnap you and it goes on for hours. They put a bag over your head and jam a gun against it. Obviously the gun isn't loaded, but it's very realistic.

They say, 'Any last words for your parents?' and 'We're going to shoot you in the face now. Is there anything you'd like to say?'

You're taught to show you're a human to get the best chance of surviving. If they see you as a relatable individual, they might hesitate before they harm or kill you.

The course was hardcore, but I didn't think I had much to worry about on this next trip. Then, a day before I was supposed to fly out to northern Iraq, I found out that the Kurdistan Prime Minister had called an independence referendum. The Iraqi Prime Minister had warned him not to, but he had gone ahead anyway, thinking it was a good moment for the Kurds to press ahead for an independent state in northern Iraq. Unfortunately it backfired and everything kicked off again massively.

Things had been really calm, but now there was a real tension between the Kurdish and Iraqi soldiers. The previous year, they had been united in the fight against Isis – and the Kurdish had been instrumental in the struggle. But as soon as they got rid of Isis, they began fighting among themselves. Skirmishes were breaking out all over the country and loads of people were being killed.

It was a really complicated situation that presented a different type of threat for us now. Our risk advisers rang and said, 'We don't think you should go today. Just wait 24 hours until we get the lay of the land.'

I couldn't believe it. My team were already out there.

I was meant to fly into Erbil but the Iraqi PM shut Erbil airport down for international flights, so I had to fly alone to Baghdad, and then from Baghdad to Erbil, where I met the team. It was madness as soon as I got there. We were staying just along the road from the American embassy where people were protesting about a land grab by the Iraqi government. The protestors were really angry and started trashing the hotel we were in, ripping down the American and Iraqi flags. It was really tense.

To complicate things, we were staying in the autonomous region of Iraqi Kurdistan but spending most of our time in Iraq, so we were having to go through a succession of road blocks to get to where we needed to film. We had two drivers: one Arabic and one Kurdish. Our Kurdish driver went up ahead through the Kurdish checks and the Arabic driver led us through the Iraqi checks.

It was scary going into Mosul, which had been under Isis control the last time I was in Iraq. I felt frightened and overwhelmed. What on earth am I doing here? I thought. It was like a nightmare. Every time I put the news on, I'd hear that another 70 people had been killed 20 miles from where we were. We were constantly having to rush filming because we were getting phone calls saying, 'We're going to close this road block in 20 minutes. If you want to come this way, you have to come now, or you will be stuck in Mosul for the night.'

We spent most of our time with Shereen, a Yazidi girl who had escaped Isis. Shereen was willing to be identified and speak out. She was pally with some of the Yazidi girls we'd met on our first trip and her story was just unbelievable.

On our first day, she took us all around Mosul. She wanted to show us where she'd been held hostage and where she had broken free. Firstly, we went to the house in east Mosul where she had been kept for months and months. East Mosul hadn't been as heavily bombed as the west of the city and the house was still standing. It was massive.

Shereen's 'owner' had been really high up in Isis. He was an executioner who put people to death on a roundabout in Mosul. She had been forced to live with this man, his wife and his parents in this house. She showed me the curtains she used to draw to try and get a bit of space and privacy. It was just so bizarre.

The parents bullied her and she was set against the wife, who became really jealous of her because the executioner had a soft spot for her. Sometimes he would say to his wife or his parents, 'Go and get Shereen. I want to have sex with her now.'

She showed me the wall where the wife had written her initials and the initials of her husband. 'Just remember, I'm the wife,' she told Shereen. 'He loves me. You're just the sex slave.'

She wasn't allowed any freedom whatsoever; she was even forbidden from going near the windows. She had no idea where she was because they'd covered her face when they drove her there. Desperate to try and get her bearings, she would stand on a stool and peep out of a tiny window in the bathroom she was allowed to use, looking in vain for mosques or shops she could identify. It was only when the family came back from shopping one day that she recognised the name of a supermarket on a shopping bag. I think I know where I am, she thought. That's how she placed herself.

Shereen was a remarkable person – really strong and sassy with quite a bit of attitude – but you would be, wouldn't you, if you'd been through all of that and stayed alive? It was extraordinary to go with her into the house where she had been abused and tortured and raped. It was the first time she'd been back.

I found it hard to comprehend what had gone on inside those walls. 'How did you find the strength to carry on?' I asked her.

'You have to believe that this day will come, that freedom will come,' she said.

Later, they moved her to a house in west Mosul. This part of the city was beyond words; it was like a horror movie. Mosul used to be a beautiful, bustling urban centre, one of the biggest cities in Iraq. Now it was pure rubble. Just imagine that happening to Birmingham, or any of our other big cities. It's unthinkable. By the end of the conflict, the Iraqi and Kurdish forces were haemorrhaging men, so to end the fighting once and for all they went all out and levelled west Mosul with rockets, street by street. There was nothing left of it.

Officially Isis had gone, but there were still Isis fighters around in sleeper cells, possibly hiding out in the network of tunnels that had been built during their occupation of Mosul. We went in with tanks on either side of us, the Iraqi forces chauffeuring us so that we didn't drive over any of the unexploded bombs Isis had deliberately left behind. They were everywhere. They had slogans written on them saying things like, 'Isis will forever be in control'.

We drove through the ruins of the city, looking for where Shereen had been kept when she was moved to west Mosul. At one point we stopped and got out of the car.

Instantly I could smell something. I looked to the right of me and there were two dead bodies in a garage. I burst into floods of tears.

'They're Isis fighters,' we were told. 'That's why no one has come to collect them.'

You could smell the flesh rotting. Shereen walked by as if nothing had happened.

'Don't go any further!' said Josh, the director. We got back in the car. 'I didn't want you to go up the road because there's a human spine up there that you don't need to see,' he explained.

It was an awful, sobering day, but, at the same time, really interesting. Shereen was delighted when we eventually found the house she had been kept in. She felt content and at peace with the fact that Isis had been destroyed and she had her freedom. Things were as they should be.

The executioner had been killed in an airstrike a few months before. We didn't know where his wife was. Although I think Shereen was glad he was dead, she wasn't full of hatred, which I think I would be if I'd been through half of what she's been through. She seemed very calm and accepting. 'He's not here now and I have my freedom,' she said. 'Some of those who should be are behind bars now. That's right and proper; that's how it should stay.'

It was incredible how strong she was. You just don't know how you would react in the same situation. The reality is that in my lifetime, we in the West have been fortunate enough not to even have to entertain that thought, because life is so comfortable. It's such a privilege not to be panicking every time you hear a bang. But if you've lived with war and conflict for years like the people of Mosul have, perhaps you become so hardened to all of the evil that's surrounding you that you just become invincible. I don't know how else to explain it.

There were still things Shereen was struggling with, though. She still had absolutely no idea where her sister was. There are loads of Yazidi girls still missing and we don't know where they are or what's happened to them. It's hard to know how many, but I suspect the number is in the thousands, and they could be dead or alive. So although Shereen is one of the lucky ones who escaped, she still has to live with not knowing where her sister is. I think that was one of the reasons she wanted to film with us, so that she could ask everyone we met, 'Have you seen this person? Do you know this name? Are there any more mass graves?'

She was determined to find answers. She was fearless and relentless. She was a real inspiration, because I was nowhere near as brave.

There are things in life you think you'll never do and then you do them and you wonder, How am I here?

Some of the worst few hours of my life were spent in a Black Hawk helicopter with the Americans, getting aerial shots of Mosul so that we could show the scale of the devastation. It was meant to be a really straightforward flight lasting an hour – up to the Mosul dam and then back down. Then, about two minutes before we were about to take off, they said, 'Oh, we've got to make a diversion to pick some of our guys up. If you want to come, you have to come now. It's not exactly what we planned, but you'll be fine. Just make sure you've got your body armour.'

'Where are we going?' I asked Helen and Josh as we threw on our bulletproof vests. There was still a part of central Iraq that Isis had control of, and since we'd been there fighting had also properly kicked off between the Kurdish and Iraqi forces.

The soldiers in the Black Hawk said, 'It's a different route and we're not exactly sure where we're going.'

I felt the panic rising. Why put ourselves in unnecessary danger? 'I don't want to be going anywhere there's any fighting,' I said. 'I just want to get the shots.'

Josh and Helen were really sweet and said, 'Look, you don't have to go if you don't want to.'

'But you can't use the shots if I'm not in them,' I said.

I put the vest on and got into the chopper thinking, What the *hell* am I doing?

The guys who were taking us up were wearing so much body armour that they looked like space warriors. All the weapons they were carrying were live and good to go, although of course they held their guns down, as is standard military practice.

It was crazy once we were in the air. I could see fighting down below – flames, fire and smoke. My heart was thumping. We were flying over a live war zone. It was really loud in the cabin and we couldn't speak to each other, so we wrote notes on our phones to communicate.

After about 90 minutes, I started to think, Something's not right. This flight is going on far longer than it should.

The soldier next to me communicated that were going to pick up two Navy SEALs.

Why are we picking up Navy SEALs if we're just going to get aerial shots of Mosul? I thought. They are the special operations part of the US Navy – proper hardcore expert soldiers who can kill anyone from anywhere.

The soldier wrote his next note in capital letters: 'STAY VIGILANT!'

I clenched my fists as we started going down, thinking, What is going on? Are we going to get shot? It terrified me that I had absolutely no control over what would happen. What can I do? I thought. I've got my vest on but I can't shoot a gun. I don't know who's coming for us, or why we're picking up Navy SEALs. I don't know why he's written 'STAY VIGILANT!' or why this flight is taking so long. And I can't ask him because I can't hear anything!

I felt sick and numb. For the soldiers, I'm sure it was pretty standard, but it wasn't my world, and I don't thrive off feeling scared. There are war journalists who buzz off that kind of adrenalin – whether they admit it or not, it gets addictive and they love feeling as if they could die at any moment. But there's no part of me that enjoys it.

After we picked up the SEALs, we flew over an IDP camp. (IDP stands for internally displaced person.) It was absolutely enormous. I thought of all of those women from Mosul who used to have careers, families, lovely houses and cars – all of it had been totally destroyed and now they were living in tiny huts. Some of the Yazidi girls were living there, too.

What was meant to be an hour's flight lasted nearly three hours. To this day, I don't know what went on. When we finally got out, I thought, I am never ever doing that again. Done!

The entire trip was like that.

Back with Shereen, we went to a court where they were trying suspected Isis fighters. Shereen and I sat in on one of the hearings. It wasn't very sophisticated – just a small sofa, a judge and a lad sat on a chair. The charge was that this lad had killed lots of people, but he was saying he hadn't. He was so tiny. He looked like a kid. If I walked past him on the street, I wouldn't fear him at all.

It was interesting to hear him talk. 'I wasn't really involved. I didn't wholeheartedly believe in anything I was doing,' he said.

It was mindblowing to be able to watch the legal process in action. It helped me to get more of a realistic picture of what the Isis organisation was like. We in the West think that everybody who's involved with Isis believes it's a just cause and a necessary fight. But for loads of these young lads, it was about being given a wage and somewhere to live. That was a revelation for me. It was circumstantial, a case of: 'You guys are in charge now, so if you ask me to build a wall, obviously I'll build a wall.'

They weren't saying, 'This is for the caliphate. We are martyrs. We are prepared to die for this.'

The fact was, there was no other way to make a living, so, 'Yes, OK, cool.'

Shereen was so poised and composed, even though she was sitting opposite an Isis sympathiser or fighter. She didn't kick off, or scream, or react in the way that you would imagine someone in her position to. She was so level headed; she asked very fair questions.

When we left the courtroom, she said, 'We need to think about maybe rehabilitating some of the kids who have been caught up in this nonsense.'

It was inspirational that she was able to be that fair and that reasonable. She just wanted to inhabit a civilised society where the Yazidis could live in peace without persecution. She wanted fairness and equality, as do all Yazidis.

There were rumours on the streets that some suspected Isis fighters had been battered to death before they got to court. Some locals told us that others were being convicted and put in prison, but then paying $20,000 to be let out. We had assumed that all of these horrific criminals were being locked up for life, but maybe not. Corruption exists everywhere, but it felt very scary.

At the end of the trip, Shereen and I went to meet a convicted Iraqi Isis killer who had been sentenced to life. He was in a maximum security prison in Sulaymaniyah in Iraqi Kurdistan.

I was worried that Shereen would find the meeting too traumatic, so I kept saying, 'If you don't want to do this, just say; if you want to leave; if you need ten minutes; anything you want, just say.'

I checked in with her again and again, the night before and on the journey to the prison. It felt like such an enormous ask to put her in front of this man. But she wanted to do it.

We arrived at the prison and were taken to a room. Shereen and I sat down. The lady in charge said, 'He'll be here in 15 minutes.'

'OK, cool,' I said.

I felt really calm at that point; I felt well equipped for the interview and confident about what we were going to ask him.

Shereen and I had been through our notes the night before. She had written down all the questions she wanted to ask in my notebook. She planned to ask him why he did it. She wanted to ask about her sister. She wanted him to know that she wasn't broken. So we felt fairly across it.

Just before he arrived, one of the Kurdish officers gave me an insight into the way Isis worked. 'These guys,' he said. 'You could walk in there not having an ounce of religion in you; give them an hour and they'd be able to persuade you to blow yourself up into millions of pieces. They are so warped. The stuff they say, the power they have and the way they are able to manipulate minds is something you've never seen before.'

What must they be saying to these young guys? I wondered.

My understanding is that a lot of the people who convert youngsters to Isis are really articulate, bright men. Often they are well-educated; they're engineers and university lecturers. Isis clearly has a sophisticated propaganda unit and anyone who underestimates these individuals is insane. People don't realise how dangerous and relentless they can be. They should not be dismissed.

I heard someone say, 'He's coming.'

Suddenly my heart started pounding, beating at a million miles an hour. This is ridiculous, I thought. Why am I feeling so nervous? There's nothing untoward here. I'm totally in control. He's going to be handcuffed. This is really, really fine.

I think it was just knowing what he had done. I was going to be sitting this close to him and it felt totally crazy. All these irrational thoughts go through your mind: What am I doing? Am I mad? Could there be repercussions? What if he gets out and comes for me?

They marched him in. There was a mask over his face so that he couldn't place which room they were taking him to. He was massive. We'd been told that he was so big when he arrived at the prison that they'd had to put two sets of handcuffs on him, because he could easily have snapped one set. He was smaller now, they said, because he'd lost lots of weight. They took his mask off. He was early twenties.

They said we could have him for an hour. Shereen spoke to him for the first 40 minutes. She asked everything she wanted to ask. Revenge isn't the right word, but it was very satisfying to be able to sit her in front of this guy so that she could have her moment. She had been bullied, dictated to and sexually abused; she'd been raped by this organisation for months and months – that was her reality. Now he was in handcuffs and wearing an orange jumpsuit. It felt like the tables had turned; it was a complete 360. She had all the power. He had no power.

That said, it was a tough interview. Halfway through, our translator, who was also from Mosul, couldn't continue because he found it so upsetting. Fortunately, the Kurdish officer jumped in and helped us out. He was a really nice guy and his English was brilliant.

Shereen seemed to be OK as she sat there, half a metre from this Isis fighter. Everyone was certain that she was going to break down, from the prison guard to the lady in charge of facilitating the interview. They were all saying, 'Don't underestimate how enormous this is for her. She might freak out or kick off or go for him.'

But she was so rational, and so dignified.

When she had finished, I had about 20 minutes with him. I thought, You know what, Stacey? It's now or never. How often are you sat face to face with someone who has affiliated themselves with such a horrific group of criminals?

I stayed calm and composed. My questions were considered. I knew anger would get me nowhere.

'Do you understand the enormity of what you've done?' I said.

He showed no remorse. He was very matter-of-fact. He guessed he had killed hundreds and hundreds of people. He had probably raped about 200 women. He had probably raped about 50 children.

'The sex felt good,' he said, 'I just couldn't stop and I didn't stop, even when the girls were begging for me to stop.'

He accepted no accountability for what he had done. He felt entitled to do it and it felt good; in his mind, it was what the women deserved. It upsets me when I think about it, because I can't imagine how frightening it must have been to have this massive guy on top of you raping you.

I was waiting for him to launch into the propaganda spiel that we're used to hearing; I fully expected him to say, 'This will get me into paradise.'

But there was none of that, which was a surprise. He said that he was a religious guy and he still prayed, but I didn't feel like he was saying, 'I'm pleased I am where I am and I wouldn't have changed anything.'

He wasn't passionate about the cause in the way some people are. I was expecting someone who would justify their actions and beliefs, but he just seemed like a young criminal who had done all of these horrific things and didn't feel any way about it. He was like an empty shell. He didn't feel human to me. He was nonchalant and aloof.

Why are you even here? I thought. Why have you agreed to speak to us?

I think it must have been out of boredom. They're in those cells every single day, so if someone says, 'Do you want the chance to have your say to an international broadcaster?' you probably would, wouldn't you? You'd kill an hour. 'Yeah, alright, cool, I'll talk to you.'

He seemed to completely accept that Isis had failed. 'They're losers,' he said. 'I did it. I was paid,' he added, which reminded me of what the lad had said at the court hearing. He was a young guy and he was in Mosul, so when Isis took over the city he had to go along with it. Suddenly their reality became everyone's reality. This is one of the big realisations

I took from my time on the ground in Iraq. Not everyone shared the absolute belief that what they were doing was right.

To a certain extent I understand, even if I don't accept, the killing. I understand that you could find yourself being told to kill or be killed; I know it goes on. If someone in a position of power says to you: 'If you don't kill him, we'll just kill you and your family,' you would probably do unimaginable things. And I think it must get to a point in your warped mind where once you've killed 50, what's another 50? Once you've killed 100, what's another 100? You become animalistic and deluded. You don't see people as humans.

It's totally insane, but I partly understood it. It was the consistent raping that got me. Because no one was telling him to do that. That was from him. It was his decision. He was evil and I felt without a doubt that he should be in prison for ever. There was no question in my mind: he was ruthless. But it was interesting, because I was also thinking, How much of a chance had he ever stood of living a normal life? When he was in his teens, his uncle blew himself up in a suicide attack in Baghdad. So that was all he'd ever really known throughout his childhood.

It was a real mind bender sitting opposite him. While I went over and over the details, I needed to focus on how Shereen was feeling, digest how I was feeling and make sure that Helen was fine and Josh had all the shots. All the while I was struggling with a deep sense of fear.

At the end of the interview, he said, 'I'm sorry if I made you feel uncomfortable talking in graphic detail about the rapes.'

No fucking way! I thought. Don't for a second think I'm going to give you the pleasure of thinking you've scared me. I will not let you walk out of this room thinking you've got the upper hand after this conversation. No chance!

'No. You don't need to apologise about that to me,' I said.

'Because you don't scare me,' I added, even though it wasn't true, 'and I can't speak on behalf of Shereen but I don't think you scare Shereen either, because the fact is she's here now and you're sat there.'

Shereen seemed really relieved after he left. She seemed much lighter as she got in the car to drive away. She had brought a pal so as to have someone familiar with her the entire time.

We had lunch that afternoon. 'Thank you so much for giving me the opportunity to do that,' she said. She seemed fine; she was on the phone to her pals. I never saw Shereen cry. She was very strong.

Although I hated being scared the whole time, I was glad that we'd gone back to Iraq and taken the chance to revisit the Yazidi community. They had made such an impression on me the first time and it was brilliant to be able to see first-hand how things had changed, a year on. We caught up with someone who could update us on the girls we had filmed fighting on the frontline, and they seemed to be doing well. They weren't fighting anymore because Isis were gone, so they were just finding their feet.

So much had changed. The war had ended in one sense but there were pockets of civil war all around. The whole landscape had totally transformed. To be able to show that, and to give Shereen her moment, was really awesome and worthwhile.

The only way is up for Shereen now, surely. Because what else could happen that hasn't already happened to her? There's nothing worse. Everything you dread, she's come through the other end of. So as far I'm concerned, she's a force to be reckoned with now. She will go on and do tremendous things, because she's not frightened. Nothing can hold her back; she will continue to grow. So that's a kind of positive to hold on to when you're around constant devastation.

Shereen reminds me a little of Nadia Murad, a Yazidi woman who was kidnapped by Isis in 2014. In 2016, Nadia became the first Goodwill Ambassador for the Dignity of Survivors of Human Trafficking at the United Nations. She is going from strength to strength, giving speeches to huge NGOs and playing an instrumental part in talking to leaders about the future of the Yazidi community and what needs to happen. She's an inspiration to all the women coming out of Iraq's chaos and conflict, including Shereen.

For now, Shereen wants to find her sister. She just needs to know what happened to her. And once she does know, she'll be able to move forward either way.

It was time to leave Iraq and, just like before, I was unbelievably relieved to get on that plane. If you haven't felt that fear, it's very hard to describe the feeling you get when you leave Iraq and fly over Europe. There's a shift in your mentality, in your body language. You exhale.

But even though this had been the most frightening, demanding documentary we'd ever made, I know it's the kind of documentary I'll be able to look back on in 25 years' time, when I'm old and washed up, and think, I'm really delighted that I pushed myself and did that.

Never again, though. And I mean it this time.

13

Fighting on

A lot of people ask me if I have a therapist. 'How are you not sliding down the walls?' they say. 'I couldn't do your job. It's so intense, so emotional.'

And it is intense and harrowing, but up until this point I haven't felt I was in a place where I couldn't deal with it myself. I'd not be embarrassed or ashamed if I did, though. I'd be the first person to pick up the phone.

One of the hardest moments of my career was seeing my first dead body in Mexico. It's difficult to see a dead body. Lots of unexpected things hit you. I wasn't expecting the smell. All these details you don't think would matter suddenly become huge in your mind. Things like her hair and her hairband – you see them every time you close your eyes. They might seem totally insignificant to somebody else, but they become enormous to you.

I suppose it's inevitable that you will hold on to those massive moments for a few weeks. People say it's healthy to go over it in your mind, but if it becomes intrusive or feels overwhelming then you should speak to someone. I dealt with it on my own.

There are many things happening in the world today that are hard to accept, especially when they have a serious impact on women and children. It helps that in my heart I truly believe without a shadow of a doubt that there are more good people than there are bad people in the world. The good definitely outdoes the bad. It's just that the evil and badness are so painful and so shocking that we have to report them. There can't be any level of tolerance. We can't accept it. And so it requires a spotlight. But there are so many really decent people trying to counterbalance the bad stuff that's going on. Some of them have had terrible experiences themselves, and that's what's brought them there. Some give up their entire lives for a cause that they believe in.

I'm thinking of the women giving out condoms to the prostitutes on the streets of St Petersburg, and warm clothes to the sex workers in Edmonton. I'm thinking of the women in NGOs all over the world who fight to get justice for battered women in Honduras, and devote their evenings to warning underage girls about pimps and predators in Japan. Then there are all the women directors, producers and fixers, and the NGOs who have hooked us up with contributors – without them there wouldn't have been any of these documentaries.

Many men have also enabled the girls in this book to have their voice. They've given them a platform and made sure they've been heard; they've given me guidance and championed women in the same way that we do. As well as directors and cameramen, I'm thinking of all the security guys over the years who have kept me safe in places like Mexico, Honduras and Iraq; all the local fixers who have hooked me up; and the drivers who drive five hours to bring a contributor to us.

It takes a huge gang of us to make sure these girls are heard – and everyone is so selfless. And actually it is inspirational to surround yourself with people who want to help others. It's a pleasure to be around kind people. You take so much away from meeting them, because you think, I'd like to be more like that. I must try to bring a bit of you with me, going forward.

The world is much more accessible now, with Twitter and Instagram and reactive news. It's a blessing and a curse, I think. Decades ago it would take time for stories to land, whereas now you're able to keep up to date and stay well informed. But we're also made aware of every single thing that feels unfair or unjust, because it's either hashtagging, trending or there have been pictures taken at the scene on someone's phone. Something can go trending within minutes of it happening.

Fake news is tricky. There are go-to media outlets that you trust, but you never know for sure. That's why I like going to locations and working out for myself on the ground what I think. There's more clarity for me if I had the conversation, somebody told me this, she showed me the scar on her tummy or she showed me a picture of her daughter. You can be more definite about what you believe.

Of course, you have a responsibility to make sure you're happy with the end result, and that can be hard. Sometimes you watch a documentary – it's your documentary, your voice and you're on the screen – and it's been cut in a way that's slightly different than what you expected.

You need to pick your battles, but you have to make sure that you're happy with the film. I'm very lucky, because my boss is such a star and I think he really respects my opinion and point of view. There has to be that level of trust. Because I was there. If they are willing to send you off, they've got to trust that you're going to do what's right and true – which, in my mind, is to raise awareness and fairly represent what's going on in the world so that people can make up their own minds about how best to fight back.

Acknowledgements

Thanks to my family, ST, Gordon Wise, Jacquie Drewe, Vanessa and Hollie, Damian Kavanagh, Danny Cohen, Gian Quaglieni, Rebecca Cripps, my amazing pals and all the INCREDIBLE crews and local fixers I've worked with over the past decade.

Forever grateful.

Picture Credits

pp. 1, 2: BBC

p6, top: Erica Jenkin/BBC

p6, bottom: Emily France/BBC

All other photos courtesy of Stacey Dooley

Index

Index

Index